The Nonprofit Board's Role in
MISSION, PLANNING, and EVALUATION

Second Edition

Kay Sprinkel Grace, MA
Amy McClellan, MNO
John A. Yankey, Ph.D.

BOARDSOURCE®
Building Effective Nonprofit Boards

Library of Congress Cataloging-in-Publication Data

Grace, Kay Sprinkel.

The Nonprofit Board's Role in Mission, Planning, and Evaluation /
Kay Sprinkel Grace, Amy McClellan, and John A. Yankey. -- 2nd ed.

   p. cm. -- (Governance series ; bk. 5)

Rev. ed. of: The nonprofit board's role in setting and advancing
the mission / Kay Sprinkel Grace. 2003; and: The nonprofit
board's role in planning and evaluation / by John A. Yankey,
Amy McClellan. 2003.

ISBN 1-58686-110-7 (pbk.)

1. Nonprofit organizations--Management.
2. Directors of corporations.
3. Boards of directors.
4. Strategic planning.
5. Mission statements. I. McClellan, Amy. II. Yankey, John A. III.
Grace, Kay Sprinkel. Nonprofit board's role in setting and advancing
the mission. IV. Yankey, John A. Nonprofit board's role in planning
and evaluation. V. Title.

      HD62.6.G713 2008
      658.4'22--dc22   2008039896

© 2009 BoardSource.
First Printing, October 2008
ISBN 1-58686-110-7

Published by BoardSource
1828 L Street, NW, Suite 900
Washington, DC 20036

BOARDSOURCE®
Building Effective Nonprofit Boards

BoardSource was established in 1988 by the Association of Governing Boards of Universities and Colleges (AGB) and Independent Sector (IS). Prior to this, in the early 1980s, the two organizations had conducted a survey and found that although 30 percent of respondents believed they were doing a good job of board education and training, the rest of the respondents reported little, if any, activity in strengthening governance. As a result, AGB and IS proposed the creation of a new organization whose mission would be to increase the effectiveness of nonprofit boards.

With a lead grant from the Kellogg Foundation and funding from five other donors, BoardSource opened its doors in 1988 as the National Center for Nonprofit Boards with a staff of three and an operating budget of $385,000. On January 1, 2002, BoardSource took on its new name and identity. These changes were the culmination of an extensive process of understanding how we were perceived, what our audiences wanted, and how we could best meet the needs of nonprofit organizations.

Today BoardSource is the premier voice of nonprofit governance. Its highly acclaimed products, programs, and services mobilize boards so that organizations fulfill their missions, achieve their goals, increase their impact, and extend their influence. BoardSource is a 501(c)(3) organization.

BoardSource provides

- resources to nonprofit leaders through workshops, training, and an extensive Web site (www.boardsource.org)

- governance consultants who work directly with nonprofit leaders to design specialized solutions to meet an organization's needs

- the world's largest, most comprehensive selection of material on nonprofit governance, including a large selection of books and CD-ROMs

- an annual conference that brings together approximately 900 governance experts, board members, and chief executives and senior staff from around the world

For more information, please visit our Web site at www.boardsource.org, e-mail us at mail@boardsource.org, or call us at 800-883-6262.

Have You Used These BoardSource Resources?

THE GOVERNANCE SERIES

1. Ten Basic Responsibilities of Nonprofit Boards, Second Edition
2. Legal Responsibilities of Nonprofit Boards, Second Edition
3. Financial Responsibilities of Nonprofit Boards, Second Edition
4. Fundraising Responsibilities of Nonprofit Boards, Second Edition
5. The Nonprofit Board's Role in Mission, Planning, and Evaluation, Second Edition
6. Structures and Practices of Nonprofit Boards, Second Edition

BOOKS

Assessment of the Chief Executive

Chief Executive Succession Planning: The Board's Role in Securing Your Organization's Future

Self-Assessment for Nonprofit Governing Boards

Transforming Board Structure: Strategies for Committees and Task Forces

Culture of Inquiry: Healthy Debate in the Boardroom

Navigating the Organizational Lifecycle: A Capacity-Building Guide for Nonprofit Leaders

The Board Building Cycle: Nine Steps to Finding, Recruiting, and Engaging Nonprofit Board Members, Second Edition

The Nonprofit Chief Executive's Ten Basic Responsibilities

Chief Executive Transitions: How to Hire and Support a Nonprofit CEO

The Board Chair Handbook, Second Edition

Getting the Best from Your Board: An Executive's Guide to a Successful Partnership

Moving Beyond Founder's Syndrome to Nonprofit Success

The Source: Twelve Principles of Governance That Power Exceptional Boards

Exceptional Board Practices: The Source in Action

Fearless Fundraising for Nonprofit Boards, Second Edition

Managing Conflicts of Interest: A Primer for Nonprofit Boards, Second Edition

Dollars and Sense: The Nonprofit Board's Guide to Determining Chief Executive Compensation

Minding the Money: An Investment Guide for Nonprofit Board members

Generating Buzz: Strategic Communications for Nonprofit Boards

Meet Smarter: A Guide to Better Nonprofit Board Meetings

The Nonprofit Policy Sampler, Second Edition

The Nonprofit Board Answer Book: A Practical Guide for Board Members and Chief Executives, Second Edition

The Nonprofit Legal Landscape

Understanding Nonprofit Financial Statements, Third Edition

The Nonprofit Board's Guide to Bylaws

DVDs

Meeting the Challenge: An Orientation to Nonprofit Board Service
Speaking of Money: A Guide to Fundraising for Nonprofit Board Members

For an up-to-date list of publications and information about current prices, membership, and other services, please call BoardSource at 800-883-6262 or visit our Web site at www.boardsource.org.

CONTENTS

ABOUT THE BOARDSOURCE GOVERNANCE SERIES

As BoardSource celebrated its 20th anniversary in 2008, we introduced updated editions of the books in the Governance Series, BoardSource's flagship series created to help nonprofit board members understand their primary roles and responsibilities. BoardSource believes that board members and chief executives who know and understand their mutual responsibilities are better equipped to advance their organizations' missions and, in turn, strengthen their communities.

WHY IS A STRONG BOARD IMPORTANT?

There's no denying that the 1.6 million nonprofit organizations in the United States play a vital role in society, from assisting victims of natural disasters to beautifying our neighborhoods, from educating our children to healing the sick. To ensure that their organizations have the resources, leadership, and oversight necessary to carry out these and other vital activities, nonprofit boards must understand and fulfill their governance responsibilities.

Although there have been headline-worthy scandals by a few nonprofits and their boards, the vast majority try hard every day to be worthy of the public's trust. Nevertheless, BoardSource frequently hears from nonprofit board members and chief executives who say that they are not always sure what the basic components of good governance are or how to educate every board member in them so they can serve their organizations and the public in the best possible manner. The revised Governance Series helps bridge this gap in knowledge.

Within the board's broad roles of setting the organization's direction, ensuring necessary resources, and providing oversight, board members wear many hats. They are guardians of the mission; they ensure compliance with legal and financial requirements; and they enforce ethical guidelines for their organization. They are policymakers, fundraisers, ambassadors, partners with the chief executive, and strategic thinkers. They monitor progress, evaluate the performance of the organization and the chief executive, and demonstrate integrity in everything they do on behalf of the organization. Because of their many roles, board members need more than enthusiasm for a cause, passion for a mission, or just "good intentions." They need to understand all of their stewardship responsibilities and perform all of their duties.

WHAT WILL BOARD MEMBERS FIND IN THE BOOKS?

The six books address all of the fundamental elements of service common to most boards, including board member responsibilities, how to structure the board in the most efficient manner, and how to accomplish governance work in the spirit of the mission of the organization.

1. *Ten Basic Responsibilities of Nonprofit Boards, Second Edition* (Book 1) by Richard T. Ingram describes the 10 core areas of board responsibility.

2. *Legal Responsibilities of Nonprofit Boards, Second Edition* (Book 2) by Bruce R. Hopkins, JD, LLM, elaborates on the board's legal responsibilities, liabilities, and the oversight it should provide to protect the organization.

3. *Financial Responsibilities of Nonprofit Boards, Second Edition* (Book 3) by Andrew S. Lang, CPA, explains board fiduciary responsibilities in the areas of financial oversight and risk management.

4. *Fundraising Responsibilities of Nonprofit Boards, Second Edition* (Book 4) by James M. Greenfield, ACFRE, FAHP, helps board members understand why they should be actively engaged in ensuring adequate resources for the organization — and how to get involved in fundraising.

5. *The Nonprofit Board's Role in Mission, Planning, and Evaluation, Second Edition* (Book 5) by Kay Sprinkel Grace, MA, Amy McClellan, MNO, and John A. Yankey, PhD, shows how to define and communicate the organization's mission and link strategic planning and evaluation to achieve organizational success.

6. *Structures and Practices of Nonprofit Boards, Second Edition* (Book 6) by Charles F. Dambach, MBA, Melissa Davis, and Robert L. Gale offers guidance on how to build and structure the board (size, committees, term limits) and enhance leadership roles and the partnership between the chair and the chief executive.

Each book focuses on one topic, breaking information into manageable amounts that are easy to digest. Readers will find real-world examples that provide insight from effective boards, statistics from BoardSource's *Nonprofit Governance Index 2007* survey of nonprofit organizations, tips and pitfalls, lists of the most important things to remember, end-of-chapter questions, glossaries, and resource lists for further reading. The authors of the books are subject-matter experts with years of experience in the nonprofit sector.

WHO SHOULD READ THE BOOKS?

Board members and senior staff, especially chief executives, in nonprofits of all types and sizes will find the information contained in the Governance Series relevant. They can use it to set standards, to develop their own approaches to board work and interacting with board members, and to modify practices as the organization evolves.

There's something in the Governance Series for everyone associated with the board. A board chair, for example, might share Book 5 (*The Nonprofit Board's Role in Mission, Planning, and Evaluation*) with board members before starting a strategic planning process or give Book 4 (*Fundraising Responsibilities of Nonprofit Boards*) to the development committee. Chief executives will find it beneficial to give Book 3 (*Financial Responsibilities of Nonprofit Boards*) to the board treasurer and to review Book 1 (*Ten Basic Responsibilities of Nonprofit Boards*) and give it, along with Book 6 (*Structures and Practices of Nonprofit Boards*), to senior staff and the board chair to clarify board–chief executive roles and strengthen the partnership with the board. All board members will want to read Book 2 (*Legal Responsibilities of Nonprofit Boards*) so they understand how to protect themselves and the organization. The chair of the governance committee might give new board members all six books. This sharing helps ensure that everyone associated with the board is "on the same page" and has a common understanding of the board's responsibilities, expectations, and activities.

Board service entails serious obligations, to be sure, but it can also deliver immense satisfaction. A board that knows what is expected of it and performs at the highest level is a strategic resource for its organization and chief executive. And ultimately, this commitment by dedicated board members translates into mission impact in our communities.

The Governance Series was made possible in part through the support of MetLife Foundation.

INTRODUCTION

LINKING MISSION, PLANNING, AND EVALUATION

> *"We have a mission statement, but we think it's a worn-out expression of what our organization is all about."*

> *"We want our mission to be more than words on our Web site, but we're not sure how to keep it front and center."*

> *"Strategic planning always takes so much time and involves so many contentious discussions. Then we create a plan, and it sits on a shelf."*

> *"We know we need to evaluate our effectiveness to maintain our credibility with stakeholders, but we don't know where to start."*

Most board members make at least one of these comments at some time during their board service. But notice that each comment isolates a particular topic: what to do about mission, or planning, or evaluation. Boards frequently tackle each as a separate issue or process. They see mission as set in stone, a statement about the organization that shouldn't be tampered with. Or they think they know what they want and need to accomplish and how they'll go about it. They assume that later on, somewhere down the road, they'll figure out if it's working. In fact, mission, planning, and evaluation are connected, and together they are a key responsibility of the board.

Mission is the "why" at the center of a nonprofit organization. A mission statement expresses the human or societal need the organization meets. The most powerful expressions of mission also incorporate language about what the organization does to meet those needs. This mission statement was developed by the staff and board leadership at WTVP public television in Peoria, Ill., as it repositioned itself for a wider role in the community and broader community investment. The statement speaks to why independent public service media are essential and then tells how WTVP fulfills that need:

> Intellectual, creative, and technological capacity is a requirement of an engaged, democratic society. WTVP uses the power of public telecommunications to inspire, enhance, and inform our community.

Mission drives visionary strategic planning, and then goals and objectives spill down from vision and are validated by mission. A regular and consistent planning process helps the board and staff clarify mission and make changes when necessary to keep mission fresh, lively, and relevant. The third ingredient in the mix — evaluation — generates the information that helps formulate goals and provides the framework for measuring those goals against mission.

This book takes an integrated approach that explains the basic principles and processes of mission, planning, and evaluation while emphasizing their interrelationship.

Chapters 1 through 4 introduce the essentials of mission. Chapter 1 defines key terms, delineates the roles of board and staff in reviewing mission, and suggests ways to know when a reassessment of mission is in order. Characteristics of a compelling mission statement are outlined in Chapter 2, along with tips for developing and expressing mission. Chapter 3 presents strategies for keeping mission visible and active. Chapter 4 recommends ways of using mission to guide board recruitment and inspire board leadership.

Chapters 5 and 6 link mission and strategic planning. Chapter 5 reviews planning, describes roles for board and staff, suggests ways to use consultants, and explains when an organization should not engage in strategic planning. Chapter 6 describes some planning approaches that work for nonprofit organizations.

Chapters 7 through 9 explain evaluation as a learning tool. They offer basic guidance about timing and benefits (Chapter 7), evaluating programs (Chapter 8), and evaluating organizational effectiveness (Chapter 9). The Conclusion summarizes key points that will help you understand and remember how mission, planning, and evaluation activities interrelate.

Discussion questions at the end of each chapter are designed to prompt board dialogue, whether at regular times set aside on the board meeting agenda; at a board retreat; or when preparing to review mission, engage in strategic planning, or conduct an organizational assessment.

What's the best reason for a board to connect mission, planning, and evaluation? Their integration provides a stronger platform for decision making. Time and money are limited resources, and nonprofit organizations need to make certain that they provide cost-effective services and programs while achieving the anticipated results.

1

CHAPTER 1

DETERMINE MISSION AND PURPOSE

The center-stage role of mission in the nonprofit sector has a strong conceptual basis. Nonprofit organizations are founded to meet a need, or a mission, and people invest time and money in these organizations to help them meet that need. People often identify first with the need and the values it represents — for example, lifelong independence; equal access to education; intelligent media; or the rights of children, seniors, or people with disabilities. They show interest in the organization's work because of its expressed mission. Trade associations or professional societies have missions related to advancing the needs of their members. Individuals or corporations join because the membership organization represents their interests and provides unique products, services, and information.

Mission in the nonprofit sector is connected to community and institutional values. While a government agency or a for-profit corporation may have a mission (and a mission statement), its mission is seldom couched in terms of values or used as a measure of performance. As part of their governance responsibilities, nonprofit board members are the keepers, watchers, challengers, revisers, and champions of the mission.

The setting and advancing of a values-based mission often stimulate lengthy discussion, generate confusion, and reveal a surprising level of institutional and individual passion about the organization and its cause. It is important to know how to channel this mission energy into an effective values-based mission expression and a positive experience for board members. Board members who know more about the function and use of mission — and how to keep it vital — more ably serve their organizations and the community.

Board members may understand that their role is to keep the mission, revisit it periodically, and be accountable for delivering on it, but they may be uncertain about how to carry out this role. They need to know three key things about working with the mission and developing mission statements:

1. Mission reflects the values, origin, and sustaining passion of the organization's very being. Discussions about mission may become quite polarized and emotional because board members may have different, but equally enthusiastic, reasons for believing in the organization's purpose. Some may be reluctant to challenge what they feel is a fundamental "truth" about why the organization exists.

2. Mission is more felt than known. Sometimes it is difficult to distill a mission into an idea and purpose that are expressed easily in a simple statement. Be patient with the process.

3. Because of the importance given to succinct expression of the mission, organizations may struggle at length with mission statements — meaning, wording, use, evaluation, and implementation — even if their sense of mission is clear.

TERMS DEFINED

Nonprofit organizations are generally described as mission driven, mission focused, and values based. A mission-driven or mission-focused organization is motivated in its programs, activities, and decision making by remembering why it exists: to meet the needs of the community. To be values based means that a set of core values inspires and guides the involvement of board members, other volunteers, staff, and donors.

Mission, vision, and values are the givens in establishing the framework for involvement, investment, and advancement of nonprofit organizations. It is essential to understand each of them.

Mission — the reason an organization exists, the need it is meeting in the community. A mission statement captures the reason and the need and adds a simple, powerful statement of what the organization is doing to meet those needs. Key questions to consider when developing a mission statement include the following:

- Does the statement clearly connect with the values of the organization?

- Is it broad enough to allow flexibility?

- Is it as succinct as possible and short enough for people to remember and repeat?

- Is it a unifying force providing direction and guidance?

Vision — what you see in the future for your community if your organization succeeds at its mission. Key questions to consider about a vision statement include the following:

- Does it challenge — make the organization reach — yet is realistic?

- Does it create passion; is it inspirational?

- Does it provide all constituencies with a clear sense of where the organization is headed and what the organization hopes to accomplish?

- Does it communicate its essential message directly and succinctly?

Values — the deeply held beliefs that guide all aspects of the organization's programs and operations and provide the litmus test for all decisions. Key questions to consider in determining values include the following:

- Do they articulate the most closely held beliefs of the organization?

- Are they defined clearly to eliminate ambiguity about their meaning in relation to the organization?

- Do they inspire pride of association?

- Do they capture the distinctive nature of the organization?

MISSION, VISION, AND VALUES: FOUR EXAMPLES

WTVP PUBLIC TELEVISION
www.wtvp.org

Mission
Intellectual, creative, and technological capacity is a requirement of an engaged democratic society. WTVP uses the power of public telecommunications to inspire, enhance, and inform our community.

Vision
Central Illinois is reinventing itself as a learning-based community. WTVP will use its technology, facilities, and creative talent to play a leading role in our region's educational, medical, economic, and cultural transformation.

Values (a selection)
We believe in the strength and the future of our community.

We believe in independence from political pressure and undue and inappropriate outside influence.

We believe that the pursuit of knowledge and access to diverse points of view are fundamental to a dynamic and informed community.

We believe the human spirit is uplifted and inspired by the arts.

We believe that lifelong learning is essential to a balanced and fair society.

We believe that strength of mind requires not only serious discourse and consideration of great ideas but also enjoyment and excitement of great entertainment.

GOODWILL INDUSTRIES OF AMERICA
www.goodwill.org

Mission
Goodwill Industries International enhances the dignity and quality of life of individuals, families, and communities by eliminating barriers to opportunity and helping people in need reach their fullest potential through the power of work.

Vision
Every person has the opportunity to achieve his/her fullest potential and participate in and contribute to all aspects of life.

Values
- Respect — We treat all people with dignity and respect.

- Stewardship — We honor our heritage by being socially, financially, and environmentally responsible.

- Ethics — We strive to meet the highest ethical standards.

- Learning — We challenge each other to strive for excellence and to continually learn.

- Innovation — We embrace continuous improvement, bold creativity, and change.

AMERICAN ASSOCIATION OF CRITICAL-CARE NURSES
www.aacn.org

Mission
Patients and their families rely on nurses at the most vulnerable times of their lives. Acute and critical care nurses rely on AACN for expert knowledge and the influence to fulfill their promise to patients and their families. AACN drives excellence because nothing less is acceptable.

Vision
AACN is dedicated to creating a healthcare system driven by the needs of patients and families where acute and critical-care nurses make their optimal contribution.

Values
As AACN works to promote its mission and vision, it is guided by values that are rooted in, and arise from, the Association's history, traditions, and culture. Therefore, AACN, its members, volunteers, and staff will

- be accountable to uphold and consistently act in concert with ethical values and principles

- advocate for organizational decisions that are driven by the needs of patients and families

- act with integrity by communicating openly and honestly, keeping promises, honoring commitments, and promoting loyalty in all relationships

- collaborate with all essential stakeholders by creating synergistic relationships to promote common interest and shared values

- provide leadership to transform thinking, structures, and processes to address opportunities and challenges

- demonstrate stewardship through fair and responsible management of resources

- embrace lifelong learning, inquiry, and critical thinking to enable each nurse to make optimal contributions

- commit to quality and excellence at all levels of the organization, meeting and exceeding standards and expectations

- promote innovation through creativity and calculated risk taking

- generate commitment and passion to the organization's causes and work

AN URBAN PRESCHOOL PROGRAM

Mission
Children need a strong start on life's learning journey. When they are guided and engaged, children eagerly embrace education. At [name of organization], we make sure that a child's first experience with learning is the successful beginning of a challenging and satisfying lifelong journey.

Vision
Our vision is that every child in the greater [city] area will be ready when it is time to start school.

Values

- Permission to learn and dream

- Education as the key to knowledge and self-confidence

- Inherent curiosity in all children

- Creating an environment for discovery

- Giving guidance in a child's first steps toward school

THE PURPOSE OF VISION AND VALUES

Your vision is your dream. Vision is the enticing idea of what could happen to the community you serve (from local to global), to the issue you address ("We envision a time when our research will have eradicated both the causes and ravages of liver cancer"), and to the organization itself if all your ideas were implemented and all your dreams came true. The vision inspires action: planning, fundraising, marketing, good governance, sound management. People want their dreams to come true.

Vision may have two parts: your vision for what your work will accomplish ("We envision a time when no child will be without health insurance and no neighborhood without health services") and your vision for your organization ("to be the most respected provider of senior services in our city"). If you only wish to express one vision, make sure it is for what the community will look like if your work is successful. Otherwise, your self-focused vision will not inspire investment or engagement.

Jane Stanford, co-founder of Stanford University with her husband, former California Governor Leland Stanford, spun out a vision for the university at a time in the early 20th century when its resources were tied up in what seemed an endless dispute over the late governor's estate. Things were so dire that she was selling her personal effects to continue paying faculty. Still, her vision persisted: "I could see a hundred years ahead, when all the present trials were forgotten, the children's children's children coming here from the East, the West, the North, and the South." Her institutional vision inspired others to keep going during a trying time in the university's history. Today, Stanford is recognized as a university of international stature.

More recently, a preschool education organization created in New Orleans to fill in where Head Start did not reach, expressed its vision well: "Our vision is that every child in the greater New Orleans area will be ready when it is time to start school."

Steve Jobs, co-founder of Apple, had a simple but global vision for the impact of his innovations on the world: "To reinvent the future." He did not express a vision for the organization but instead for the way in which his organization would change technology. He was right.

Values are embedded in both mission and vision. Values are what click with people when they read an organization's materials. Vision statements also have implicit and expressed values. As boards work to gain a sense of mission and to create and reaffirm mission statements, it is imperative to know and communicate values.

One seasoned corporate executive, when asked to define what values meant to his involvement as chair of a nonprofit science center's board, said they were his deeply held beliefs that inspire and guide both his involvement and outreach. He listed these beliefs as discovery, fiscal responsibility, education, and accessibility. That mix illustrates the wide range of values that board members, other volunteers, and donors may express.

People are drawn to organizations whose values they share. They seldom work for, give to, ask for, join, or serve organizations whose values they do not share. An organization's ability to embed values in its mission is key to attracting board members, volunteers, staff, and donors who want to support organizations working on the issues that are most important to them. Expression of those values in the beginning of a mission statement will attract people's interest in a way that the description of what the organization does cannot.

People weigh an organization's performance by the way it acts on its professed values, makes an impact in the community, and lives up to its mission. This is particularly true of those new to philanthropy — younger donor-investors, women with earned wealth, people with new wealth from the intergenerational transfer of assets, and members of ethnic groups previously underrepresented in philanthropy. These newer donors have led many organizations to re-examine not only what they are doing and how they are doing it but also why. They come to the practice of giving, joining, and serving with fresh eyes and new standards. Their involvement has led to long-overdue Web site design and content reform, especially as social networking software becomes available to nonprofit organizations and associations. Attracted by what they read and hear, these new donors are aligning and mobilizing their friends to support organizations through small gifts and viral marketing. There is greater scrutiny as we move outside the circles of more traditional donors. As a result, boards are expected to be transparent; accountable; and rigorous in their evaluation of mission, values, and performance.

As important as a values statement can be to an organization's strategic direction, it does not take the place of a code of ethics — a document describing a code of conduct for board and staff. With its explicit guidance about actions, behaviors, and decision making, a code of ethics sends a message about the culture and work of the organization.

For more information on codes of ethics, see *Legal Responsibilities of Nonprofit Boards*, Book 2 in the BoardSource Governance Series.

TIP

Provide regular opportunities for discussing, reviewing, and assessing your mission. Build "mission moments" into board meetings by inviting a satisfied constituent or audience member to make a five- to 10-minute presentation on the organization's impact. Plan board retreat sessions devoted to examining mission through longer community impact presentations.

MISSION ROLES FOR BOARD AND STAFF

Determining and advancing the mission is not only a key job for board members. It is also a focal point for the constructive partnership between board and staff. Board members represent the community and therefore bring vital perspectives that help determine the need to be met by the organization.

Some board members will want to become closely involved in determining the mission. While this involvement is motivating for some, others will be content with providing critique and feedback on the final product. Board members who are keenly interested in both the process and the product should take the lead, in collaboration with staff, concerning mission development and then share their thoughts with the entire board for discussion and final approval.

Boards of organizations that operate with a mission defined by a founder or a founding board have a special responsibility in mission development. These organizations may evolve so that the founder's mission and vision have served their purpose well but are no longer as current or effective as they could be. The board's task is to reassess the validity of the mission — and revise it if necessary — to ensure that it remains fresh and reflective of the needs the organization is meeting.

Because staff members, paid and volunteer, implement the mission and make daily decisions about programs and services that reflect the mission, they also need to play a pivotal part in developing the ideas and statement that will guide their work. Resentment arises when a well-intentioned board simply thrusts an idea or statement on staff without the latter's true involvement. And when boards operate without staff input, ownership of the ultimate mission statement is limited. (Of course, the converse is true as well: The board will have limited ownership of a mission statement developed without its input.)

Be sure that staff leaders (program, administration, marketing, fundraising) contribute to any process of creating, revising, or reviewing the mission statement. They bring a valuable internal perspective to the process, including familiarity with the organization's clients, members, or constituents and knowledge of other organizations that provide similar or complementary services. That knowledge helps sharpen and refine the way in which the mission is expressed — capturing the uniqueness of focus and services.

PITFALL

When the board doesn't have mission in mind, day-to-day issues can dominate at the expense of the larger "why" and "what" of the organization. When the mission is no longer viable, the organization's ability to engage others and stay financially stable will be at risk.

WHEN TO EVALUATE MISSION

As the most enduring aspect of an organization, mission should not be tampered with or changed without the serious involvement of staff, board, key donors, and representative members of the community. It should not be altered or discarded without an extensive review of the organization, the external environment, and the specific community the nonprofit serves.

The best way to know whether mission, vision, and values need evaluation is to conduct a periodic review. Even if the board and staff do not anticipate altering these statements, a review offers a good opportunity to recommit to the organization's fundamental purpose. There are several ways to go about it:

1. Appoint a task force that meets once or twice annually to review the mission ("We exist because..."), vision ("Our vision for our community is..."), and values (deeply held beliefs that guide decision making both within the organization and for the community). These task force sessions — scheduled in advance of the full board's annual review of the strategic plan — uses the year's accomplishments and practices as the litmus test.

   One public television station followed this approach, evaluating its programs (televised and community) against its mission, vision, and values. The exercise was interesting and engaging, and it involved clarifying the "fit" of some programming. As a result, the group concluded that some programming was perhaps not sufficiently aligned and should be re-evaluated.

2. Conduct a "market survey" of donors, using SurveyMonkey or another online survey with those who have given the organization e-mail addresses. The survey can use multiple-choice questions to test the inference of donors against the stated mission of the organization. Sometimes the results are quite surprising; sometimes they are very reinforcing. Review the survey with the board before putting it online, and bring the results to the board for discussion. If there are insufficient e-mail addresses to constitute a good sample, then regular mail can be used.

3. Review the mission, vision, and values at a board meeting. Distribute the statements before the meeting with the board packet, and provide guiding questions for members to think about in advance. Be sure to dedicate enough time on the agenda — at least 45 minutes — to a full discussion of the three statements.

Seldom does the review lead to a change in mission. Sometimes the vision is revised, particularly if it has been too organization-focused, and usually the values remain intact.

Eventually, every organization needs a more serious evaluation. You'll know when it's time to evaluate whether the mission remains valid and relevant if

- the reason for an organization's existence has faded from the community's needs

- the need has been met

- another organization now exists that is meeting this need more effectively

- significant new opportunities have arisen that prompt a rethinking of the mission on a deeper level

- A split has emerged among the leadership or members as to the fundamental mission and direction of the organization

The March of Dimes provides one well-known example of an organization that met its original mission. It was created to provide funding for research and treatment of infantile paralysis (poliomyelitis/polio), but its own research and the development of the Salk and Sabin vaccines in the 1950s and 1960s nearly eradicated polio as a threat in most parts of the world. Rather than go out of business, the March of Dimes looked for another need to meet and found that no other organization with its reach and recognition had the elimination of birth defects as its mission. Reinvented, the March of Dimes has successfully raised large amounts of money and visibility for its new mission.

The mission and the expression of the mission must remain dynamic and connected to a viable organization that is meeting an important community need. One outcome of mission evaluation every several years is to determine whether an organization still has a reason to exist. If it does not, it should not. When boards and staffs become so attached to the organizational entity that they cannot accept the reality of a mission that has been accomplished (or is being better met by another organization), great difficulties arise in marketing, fundraising, and community recognition.

It has been said that in an ideal world — one in which chronic and acute diseases, domestic or social violence, and the other critical issues in our communities have been eradicated — nonprofits would exist only to enrich our educational, spiritual, and cultural lives. What a fine dream! However, for most communities, such a day will probably never come. Therefore, nonprofit organizations must attend to mission: identifying the need they must meet and then creating, advancing, articulating, and evaluating a values-based mission that will move them toward solving and serving the issues of importance to our communities.

QUESTIONS THE BOARD SHOULD ASK

1. Does every board member know our mission statement by heart?

2. Does our organization have a vision statement? If not, why?

3. Does our organization have a values statement? If not, why?

4. Are we clear about board and staff roles in relation to mission development?

5. Do we review our mission periodically at a board retreat?

CHAPTER 2
DEVELOPING AND EXPRESSING MISSION

The nonprofit mission statement expresses the "why." It describes the need that is being met and what the organization is doing to meet it. A mission statement that inspires involvement and keeps board and staff motivated is rare. Mission statements have both an internal and an external purpose: Internally, they remind and inspire board and staff; externally, they attract people to the cause.

A compelling mission statement tends to have nine characteristics.

1. It uses bold, clear, and memorable language.

2. It conveys the organization's values both explicitly and implicitly.

3. It has both an emotional and a rational impact.

4. It combines a "why" statement with a "what" statement.

5. It describes the need being met in positive, not negative, terms.

6. It uses verbs that are active, not passive.

7. It inspires people to act, give, join, serve, learn more.

8. It can be adapted for both marketing and development.

9. It summarizes the mission succinctly.

A vision statement is something different: It is the expression of what you see in the future if your organization is successful at addressing its mission. You need both a vision and a mission. The vision provides the inspiration for the organization's plan. It is the destination, and the plan is the road map. The mission is the compass — the true north for the organization, the point on which there is full agreement. It serves as the tiebreaker when needed and guides an organization along the right path.

NOT JUST WHAT, BUT WHY

Board members whose experience is rooted in the corporate world will be more comfortable with mission statements that focus on the what: "The mission of XYZ organization is to provide programs and services for those who suffer from hunger." The more powerful kind of mission statement, however, focuses on the why.

In the nonprofit sector, why becomes the critical question because we are engaging people at the level of their deepest values and asking them to provide time and financial support for which the only return on investment is the knowledge of how they are making a difference. Coupling the why with a simple what statement usually satisfies the needs of those who want to see a more traditional corporate statement.

As an example, an organization that works with people who have sustained injuries to their hands created a powerful example of a mission statement combining the why with the what:

> Next to the human face, hands are our most expressive feature. We talk with them. We work with them. We play with them. We comfort and love with them. An injury to the hand affects a person professionally and personally. At XYZ Organization, we give people back the use of their hands.

Although this mission statement can stand alone, it was also ably incorporated throughout the organization, with minor wording changes, using compelling design and graphics. It appeared on the cover of a brochure and in other materials, accompanied by program descriptions, successful treatment and therapy stories, goals of the organization, and other supporting information.

Nearly two decades ago, the Yale University School of Medicine developed this mission statement for a large capital campaign:

> We are in the midst of one of the most profound intellectual revolutions of all time, the revolution in the biological sciences. Its implications for understanding life's processes and for combating disease are boundless. Yale is in the forefront of this revolution.

The language is bold, the values are implicit, the impact is both emotional and rational, the why and what are both present. The statement is positive, active, inspirational, and a succinct summary of the mission. In developing this statement, Yale University School of Medicine captured the capital campaign opportunity yet tied it implicitly to the idea that Yale, with its reputation and experience, was going to lead the way. Directed for the most part at those connected to Yale and to the medical profession, this mission statement served as both a call to action and an invitation to join with others who were doing important work.

Too often, mission statements end up expressing what the organization does without explaining *why* the services are necessary. A simple, two-step exercise conducted at a board meeting, board–staff retreat, or other appropriate gathering helps identify the why:

1. Ask those present to answer the question "Why do we exist?" Tell them they cannot use the infinitive form of the verb (to educate, to provide, to counsel, etc.).

2. If they struggle with this task, ask them to finish this sentence: "We exist because…." Ask them to describe the need the organization is meeting.

A food bank, struggling with too much description of what it did and too little articulated about why, came up with this: (We exist because) "Hunger hurts." The organization expanded the idea that hunger hurts not only the individuals who experience it but also the communities in which they live through diminished productivity, social challenges, and inability to access their full potential.

Although the food bank chose not to use "We exist because hunger hurts" as its official mission statement, preferring a "what" statement instead, the senior development officer began incorporating the new statement into her community outreach talks and materials as they launched a capital campaign. It was compelling, provocative, and effective.

TWO "WHY" MISSION STATEMENTS

1. A science museum that has extensive programming and exhibits geared to both children and adults, and that prides itself on being interactive and accessible, developed a mission statement for a capital campaign. The brochure was itself innovative: It had a plain pebble gray cover with only the name of the institution, and it carried a two-by-two-inch plastic bag that contained a piece of flint, a computer chip, a piece of foil, and a bird feather — all scientific artifacts. Inside the front cover, at the top, appeared these words:

   From ancient chipped stone tools to modern computer chips, ingenuity is the human signature. We seek to understand and mimic a world and universe in which we are newcomers, to fly with birds, to communicate at the speed of light. This scientific quest is written in things we can touch, each of them a window to the future.

   At the XYZ Science Museum, we touch the future, hands-on.

   The brochure then went directly into the experience that awaited visitors, written in language that made them feel as though they were there. It was a clear statement of the mission (the needs the organization was meeting) as well as the impact (the difference it was making in the community).

2. An organization that provides consultation and resources to people who are deaf or hard of hearing wanted to create a new mission statement. A core team of six people from the board and staff, working with a consultant, created a trial mission statement that was tested with several

constituencies before it became final. The process included probing the "why" at length, identifying key values, agreeing about tone and language, and then putting phrases together that expressed "why."

> We exist in a world of sound: children's voices, laughter and music, a baby's cry, the echo of fog horns, crunching leaves, a crackling fire, words of love and reassurance, whispered thoughts, soft breathing in the night, the ringing of a phone, signals of danger, and the fun of casual conversation.

> Hearing loss separates us from these sounds. ABC Association helps people reconnect.

From this, the association drew a tagline for its stationery and brochures: *Reconnecting people with their world.*

SUGGESTIONS FOR DEVELOPING MISSION

Few processes can get as bogged down as identifying mission and developing the mission statement. It is essential to focus on the substance of the mission before trying to write a statement. Here are five ideas to ensure a productive process and a strong result.

1. Don't begin by trying to write something. Focus first on the mission itself. In the process of identifying and expressing the mission, the tendency is to look at the organization — to gaze into mirrors and try to figure out what the organization is, what it should be doing, and how it needs to do it. Instead, first look through windows into the community. What does the community need? What population does the organization want to serve and why? How can the need(s) be described, and how can the organization be defined? What kinds of programs will be developed to meet those needs?

   A venerable land conservation organization, making a major transition in leadership, initiated its planning process by doing a market survey and then evaluating its mission statement against what it was hearing from the stakeholders. As a result, the organization evaluated everything from its name (keeping its original one, but becoming more dedicated to it for having questioned it) to its mission statement, which it improved significantly. Once the scan of the community was completed and the needs were described, the organization looked internally and defined the resources that would be needed to serve the mission. The result was a strong plan, a revised mission statement, and a new leader who was energized by the action the board had taken.

2. Ensure that board members and the chief executive agree on the mission. Much of the confusion, dissension, disaffection, and turmoil that characterize dysfunctional nonprofits stems from disagreement about the mission. Because mission should ultimately define program development, decision making, policy setting, fundraising strategy, and all other related board actions, it is essential to have a common understanding of the mission.

Problems arise when the mission is not used often enough in institutional decisions and evaluations. Organizations that go on cruise control and never really engage the board in discussions or evaluations of organizational issues related to mission may find themselves experiencing mission drift. In this acute but preventable condition, boards become so disconnected from the mission (the world outside the windows) that they obsessively focus on the organization itself (the world limited to what can be seen in the mirror). With mission development and advancement, the process is as important as the product.

3. Keep the mission visible, robust, nimble, and relevant. If the mission is reviewed regularly, and if all board meetings have a mission moment (or two) that demonstrates the organization's connection with stakeholders, the potential for mission drift diminishes dramatically. Without a connection to why the organization exists, board members can leave meetings with knowledge only of financial windfalls or shortfalls, personnel changes, capital needs, fundraising plans, and committee reports.

Schedule a mission moment during the middle of each board meeting. Invite someone whose life has been touched by what you do to give a short, personal testimonial: a client or client family, a grateful patient, a satisfied symphony patron, or kids who love camping. Here are some examples of effective mission moments:

- At a learning disability center for children, a teacher from the school district came to tell the board what a difference she saw in the learning skills development among children who had been in its programs.

- At a medical center, members of a patient's family came to thank the board for creating the hospice program that had provided comfort and support for their grandmother and the entire family.

- At a baroque orchestra, musicians from the orchestra came to each board meeting over a year's time to explain more about their rare and unusual instruments and to give a short concert.

- At a nurses' association, a nurse discussed how the changes in accreditation requirements have improved the quality of care in her hospital.

If you want board members to leave meetings with light in their eyes and enthusiasm on their lips — ready to raise funds, recruit new board members, and just generally spread the good news about your mission — then be sure that every meeting gives them something to talk about. They will repeat the stories they hear from these satisfied customers to family, Rotary, barber, grocery clerk, pharmacist, friends, and professional colleagues. The mission will become better known, and so will the organization. Mission moments also work well at staff meetings to connect staff members with the impact of their work in the community.

MISSION DRIFT

Mission drift is a condition, either long term or temporary, in which an organization becomes so consumed with its (internal) institutional issues that it loses sight of its mission. A popular cartoon several decades ago showed a man, with only his head visible, being sucked into quicksand and surrounded by alligators. The caption read, "When you are up to your neck in alligators, it's hard to remember that the original mission was to drain the swamp."

The most common source of mission drift is a deterioration of leadership, which leads to a crumbling of systems within the organization. The organizational focus shifts from strategies for meeting community needs to tactics for controlling internal problems. Symptoms that may indicate mild to severe mission drift are

- board meetings in which there is little or no mention of the programs or services except in the financial statements

- board members who refuse to get involved with the organization except at board meetings and make little or no financial commitment

- leaders who fail to encourage leadership growth and succession

- battle for control between board and staff

- an approach to organizational priorities that ignores the needs of constituencies and changes in the marketplace

- a shift from the passionate commitment that characterizes board membership in an organization at its founding or early stages to an overly pragmatic view often found among board members in organizations with greater maturity

- initiatives that go beyond the normal scope of the organization's activities

- a lack of strategic focus as a regular element of board meetings

- a lack of accountability and criteria for success when evaluating programs

- staff or board members expressing concern that the organization is diverting from its core purpose

Any of these symptoms is dangerous and can damage an organization's capacity to enroll others in its mission and stay financially stable. Each should be addressed as it arises and dealt with decisively. All detract from the required emphasis on mission and can overly divert attention to organizational issues rather than program accomplishments. Uncontrolled, these problems can become so consuming that the organization ends up getting in the way of the mission.

Adapted from Kay Sprinkel Grace, *Beyond Fund Raising: New Strategies for Nonprofit Innovation and Investment, Second Edition* (John Wiley & Sons, Inc., 1997, 2005). Reprinted with permission.

4. Offer opportunities for longer mission interaction. Board retreats, board–staff retreats, and community events all offer good opportunities to convey mission. New board or staff members have a chance for immersion in mission through presentations by an organization's clients. External mission moments inspire the public; lay the groundwork for mission-based advocacy, fundraising, and outreach; and create pride among the board members who are present. Here are a few examples:

- An organization that provides guide dogs for blind and sight-impaired people invites several owners and their dogs to come to a board retreat and tell how having the dogs has made a difference in their lives. The board chair also reads two letters from individuals who could not attend but wanted to express their gratitude.

- A family foundation plans an annual board retreat in a city where a major grantee is located and incorporates a site visit into the retreat agenda. The direct contact between the grantor and the grantee is a mutually beneficial way to share information and see the effects of the funding.

- An organization raising money for child-care scholarships invites recipients to make brief presentations at a board retreat. This improves the board's understanding of why the scholarship funds are important and need to be raised.

- An organization that provides residencies for working artists holds an annual open house where board members, donors, and their guests become immersed in the joy of these artists who have been given the "gift of time." Guests are inspired to get involved, and board members and donors reconnect with why they have made their commitment.

5. Consciously use mission as the basis for making tough decisions. A focus on mission is critical when expanding a program, maintaining a program that is a financial drain but essential to mission, deciding that the chief executive is not keeping pace with community changes that affect program delivery, or making the annual report format more cost-effective.

In one organization, the renewed sense of mission helped a board make a tough decision about raising additional endowment monies so that some existing endowment funds could be used to purchase property that was critical to program delivery. After several negative no-resolution board meetings, the chief executive skillfully reconnected the board with the mission. She brought board members to the site so they could experience the impact of their summer day camp programs on underserved children. With the mission on display, the decision suddenly became easy to make.

☼ PITFALL

Although defining the mission requires the interaction of various stakeholders, having a committee actually draft the statement is a sure way to create something cumbersome or diluted. Group action for the writing task always proves an obstacle to clarity and succinctness.

WRITING A MISSION STATEMENT

Here is a suggested process for tackling the challenging job of writing (or revising) the mission statement. Many organizations have used this process to clarify values, promote ownership of the final product, and ensure an appropriate level of board participation.

1. Identify (or reaffirm) values. Start by defining (or re-examining) the values (deeply held beliefs) that guide your mission. Involve board and staff in the process at a special meeting or at a board meeting to which staff leaders are invited. Ask each board and staff member to write down three values he or she believes are basic to the organization.

   For a seniors' organization that provides home care to keep people out of nursing homes, for example, the list may include dignity, independence, caring, nurturing, cost-effectiveness, longevity, and quality of life. Or, if your organization provides educational programs to children living in poverty, your list may include opportunity, hope, realizing potential, knowledge, and the future.

   After everyone creates a list of three or more values, have each person read his or her list to the rest of the group and capture the words on a single easel sheet or computer screen projection program. When duplication of words occurs (which it should and will), note the number of times a value word is given.

2. Discuss these values. Be sure everyone understands the meaning of each word or phrase. Let people explain what they mean: Often the explanation is richer than the word or words themselves. Add to the list if people think of others. See what is missing.

3. Appoint a creative team. If you are creating a mission statement for the first time, assign a small board and staff team of creative thinkers and writers to work with the values words and with other descriptive material about your organization in order to write one or more short, powerful mission statements that embody the key values.

Before sending the team off to do its work, read examples of mission statements — ranging in tone from poetic to corporate — and see which style the board feels is most appropriate for your organization.

4. Respond to a draft. Have the team bring the first draft to a board meeting, but don't engage in wordsmithing. Ask board members to respond to the intent, tone, and general message, as well as the overall impact of the language — but not to details of wording. Ask for both verbal and written feedback.

   Take time at the board meeting to collect all suggestions, or the responses will trickle in (or not come at all) and the process will be delayed. With this feedback, either return the information to the board members (and possibly a staff member or two) assigned to the mission statement, or hand off the process to a professional writer for final polishing.

5. Bring the final draft version to the board for preliminary approval. If anyone raises serious objections (missed the point, wrong tone for our organization, too negative, too flowery, too corporate), address them. If the objections are in the form of wordsmithing from people who did not use earlier opportunities for critical input, then deal with them graciously, but don't derail the process. If the editorial criticisms have merit, consider them.

6. Before adopting the mission statement, let it rest for a while and test it out with others. Put the mission statement aside momentarily and make sure that it gels. During this time, send the proposed statement, stamped DRAFT, to a few key volunteers and donors and ask for their input and reaction. Engage them in a brief conversation about what the new draft mission statement says to them. Even if they don't respond, they will remember that you involved them in the process.

   Circulate the draft statement among staff. Try using it in some materials, and see how you like it as an organization. Post it on the wall, and have members, clients, or patrons respond. Think hard about your mission and values, and make sure that both are incorporated. Sometimes it is easy to get caught up in the rhythm and words — particularly if a statement is well written — and later realize that the content does not exactly reflect the why and the values.

7. Approve the new mission statement. As the statement is used, you may receive additional feedback. Make note of it, and refer to that feedback when the time comes to evaluate the statement. Have the board officially adopt the mission statement with the understanding that all other forms of the mission statement will no longer be used except in a historical context.

TIP

Before writing a concrete mission statement, step back. Focus first on the mission itself by looking into the community. What does the community need? How can that need be met?

A MISSION SUCCESS STORY

It is one thing to know the mission; it is quite another to find language that people will agree on. Board members of an environmental education organization struggled through many meetings debating fine points of wording in the mission statement. No one could resolve the differing interpretations in the room, and the discussion was at a standstill.

Then one board member suggested a completely new approach to creating an accurate and compelling mission message. Instead of trying to generate the mission internally through countless hours of board discussion, the organization asked its customers — those who hiked on the property, those who brought children to day camp, those who bought fresh produce or visited the farm animals — what they felt the mission or purpose of the organization was. The answers gave the board the inspiration it needed to go beyond its semantic stalemate and revitalized the board members' sense of why they were involved.

Customer feedback centered around one key idea that framed the eventual mission statement: This organization teaches young people and other visitors the importance of being good stewards of the planet. All it took to find the right language was to stop talking internally about words and start inquiring externally about ideas and values.

QUESTIONS THE BOARD SHOULD ASK

1. Does our mission statement incorporate the sense of "why" of our organization?

2. Do we integrate the mission into every meeting, gathering, and function?

3. How do we give board members the opportunity to observe the mission in action?

4. How do we respond when we see signs of mission drift in our organization?

CHAPTER 3
ACTIVATING AND ADVANCING MISSION

The challenging work of developing a mission and articulating it in a written mission statement is just the beginning. Mission must be fresh, visible, and active — not just an eloquent statement with good intentions.

Internally, the mission inspires and motivates the board and the staff. One of its most significant and visible internal uses, as later chapters in this book will explain, is as a guidepost for planning and evaluation. Externally, mission is just as critical because it expresses the need that the organization meets. In the community, a consistent effort to share the mission is essential to successful advocacy, marketing, and fundraising.

MISSION AS INSPIRATION AND MOTIVATION

On the tourist map of the nonprofit sector, mission and its expression should be Inspiration Point. While it's tempting to think the most important use of the mission statement is in reaching out to the community, remember that those closest to the heart of the organization need to feel motivated, too. If board members are to be keepers of the mission, they need to understand how it drives their decisions, their eagerness to involve others, and their willingness to support it financially. If staff members don't stay invigorated by their reasons for doing what they do, they will lose interest in what they are doing.

It is easy to get distracted from mission. Daily crises overwhelm energy and spirit as people become caught up in overwork, stress, disappointments, challenges, and frustrations. When that happens, get reconnected with the mission. Go visit the reason why you raise money: the disabled children, frail seniors, rehearsing musicians, school children being tutored, the preserved forest, the religious service in the new building.

Immerse yourself in the experience, and know the impact of what you do and the importance of the mission you are serving.

If you are a board member, take a staff member with you; if you are a staff member, invite a board member along. Use mission moments at board and staff meetings as often as practical, and ask to see correspondence from satisfied clients, members, or visitors. Then reread your mission expression; see how it captures what you have seen and felt. You will find yourself becoming inspired and energized. And if you don't, then perhaps the mission itself does not inspire you, and you should rethink your own involvement.

MISSION AND STRATEGIC PLANNING

While the vision (the big dream) stimulates goals, the mission (implicit and written) provides the ultimate litmus test for program decisions. Strategic thinking as well as the strategic planning process involves refining the vision into goals and the goals into objectives. If the vision is the destination and the plan the road map, then the mission is true north. Check your direction by looking at the mission. Here's an example:

> *Vision:* In our community, seniors of all abilities and their caregivers will enjoy the highest possible level of service and independence.

> *Goal* (one of several): To create Alzheimer's day care centers in neighborhoods not currently served

> *Objective:* By July 2009, board and administrative staff to identify an additional two sites for future Alzheimer's day care centers and begin developing plans for their creation

Imagine that a board and staff, in their strategic planning process, have created several goals and many objectives to support these goals. At some point, these goals and objectives need to be checked against the mission: Why does this organization exist? Now imagine that the mission was more focused on home health care for the frail elderly and that other organizations were providing Alzheimer's day care. Imagine that the underlying values were independence, dignity, and quality of life. The organization would have to take a serious look not only at its mission but also at its resources to determine whether it needed to expand in this area.

Every strategic planning process should begin with a review of the mission. Conduct a scan of the environment (outside the windows) to determine whether the need the organization is meeting is still the most critical need. An environmental scan is an information-gathering process — using research, surveys, and interviews — that asks what critical external issues the organization needs to address and what problems its clients and stakeholders face.

One children's health organization, formed in the early 1950s by a pediatrician with the help of community leaders, primarily focused on two neglected areas in children's medical services: mental retardation and post-polio physical therapy. Shortly after the organization's founding, another group, part of a national organization, moved into the community and had a greater reach and visibility for its programs for developmentally challenged children. At the same time, the development of the Salk and Sabin vaccines dramatically diminished the threat of polio to children.

Rather than continue trying to meet the organization's original mission in this changing environment, the board and founder looked into the community for other needs in children's health. They determined that the hidden handicaps that children suffered — educational, emotional, neurological, and language disabilities — remained largely unmet. They created a new strategic plan and shifted their programming to meet the new needs they had discovered as their mission. Now, nearly 50 years later, the organization is still thriving. Interestingly enough, the organization kept its original mission-based tag line: New futures for multi-handicapped children.

Follow the guidance in this book — especially Chapters 5 and 6 — for a mission-driven approach to strategic planning. In the written plan, be sure to feature both your vision and your mission in the opening section. As a reference point, this section will help board and staff implement and evaluate the plan effectively.

MISSION AND ADVOCACY

As a way of building understanding and support, getting the mission out into the community is a key responsibility of nonprofit boards. Here are some places and platforms where the mission can be shared:

Electronic and print communications. Posting the mission statement on your Web site is just the beginning. Add dimension to the mission with changing images and stories about the organization's impact. One organization, in a building program and still raising money, had an engaged board member who flew over the construction site in his plane once a week and took aerial digital photographs, which he posted on the Web site. Be sure that your Web site (which should always be current) emphasizes your impact. People give to the community through organizations. They want to know that their investment has made a difference.

In your newsletter and in e-mails to supporters, members, and constituents, share good news about a client success, community recognition, or staff achievement, and include the way in which this advances the mission of your organization. Invest in print and electronic materials — design, photography, and writing — that carry powerful messages about mission and values through images and words. Periodically, review organizational materials to be sure they reflect mission and values.

Community forums. Opportunities to speak at churches, service clubs, and other forums are another avenue for both board members and staff to spread the meaning of an organization's mission in the community. For example, the food bank mentioned in Chapter 2 launched an ambitious capital campaign and found a dramatic use for its "Hunger hurts" statement. Although the board was not keen on the theme, the development director was undaunted. Widely sought as a speaker, she incorporated the statement as the opening of her speeches in the community. She would begin her talk by looking out at the satisfied audience — happily digesting their lunch or dinner — engaging their eyes and then their attention by simply saying, "Hunger hurts." Her talk focused not on the food bank's fundraising needs but on the needs the food bank was meeting. The campaign was a huge success.

Informal advocacy. When board and staff understand and embrace the mission and mission statement, they can talk easily about the organization and its impact. Among family, business colleagues, and friends, people's enthusiasm is contagious when they focus on the need their organization is meeting.

Equipping board and staff members with success stories and a two-minute "elevator speech" about the organization goes a long way to promote their comfort with informal advocacy. The elevator speech exercise is a good one for board and staff meetings: Imagine that you get on an elevator and run into an old friend who asks you what you're doing or what you're involved in. The friend presses the button for the 10th floor, and there are two other stops. What's the most effective message about the organization that you can deliver in that short time? The "elevator question" is another important tool. Don't let your friend get off the elevator without saying, "I am so pleased with your interest. I would love to have you come for a tour sometime. May we arrange that?" Then the contact is not lost. Business cards are exchanged, and the process has begun.

MISSION AND MARKETING

Nonprofit organizations could learn something from corporations about using their values and mission as marketing tools. Car companies emphasize how young, popular, alive, and excited you'll feel by buying one of their automobiles — while telling little about the car itself. Ice cream producers say you *deserve* to indulge in their product, and one insurance company ran a memorable series of print ads that mentioned little about insurance. One ad featured an eye-catching drawing of a woman with wild hair, standing on a rooftop in a tornado. The text read, "Life is like a tornado watch. You can hide in the basement until it's over, or you can stand on the roof, get rock star hair and shout, 'I knew you were coming; that's why I didn't rake the leaves!'" Only the company logo at the bottom of the page indicated what the ad was really about.

Admittedly, corporations use marketing statements, not mission statements. However, nonprofits can use their mission statements as the centerpiece for marketing — for engaging the community as volunteers, participants, and investors. One independent school integrated its values and mission into its enrollment marketing as well as into its fundraising materials. The language was powerful and values based:

> Welcome to ABC School, where students, parents, and teachers are creating a new kind of high school. Rigorous and rewarding, committed to diversity, deeply connected to our community — ABC is where remarkable students are growing into the leaders of tomorrow.

The enrollment marketing tagline was simple and compelling: "The tradition begins with you." The school met its enrollment goals and, using the same values-laden language, raised funds in a successful campaign to build a new campus.

For a medical center, the mission statement may be incorporated into community marketing to increase hospital use. For a church, marketing may be aimed at increasing attendance at services or enrollment in the day or religious school. For an organization like Planned Parenthood, marketing may be focused on teen educational programs or women's clinics. In their marketing materials, trade and professional associations may focus on the improved employment opportunities for members who attend the annual conference.

MISSION AND FUNDRAISING

Fundraising once was considered a tin-cup exercise in which dedicated volunteers and staff members went out into the community and talked about the organization's need for money. Attitudes have changed, but board members still can be less than enthusiastic about this aspect of their responsibilities. In fact, respondents to BoardSource's *Nonprofit Governance Index 2007* ranked fundraising as the number one area of board performance needing improvement. Often suffering from a fear of fundraising, board members say they feel more comfortable with asking indirectly by writing letters or providing names and addresses of potential donors; they are less eager to make phone calls or ask for money face to face.

Using a mission-driven approach can help alleviate fear of fundraising, in part because it gives board members new terms and new approaches to use. When organizations ask for community support because they meet needs, not because they have needs, the tin cup disappears, and the fear dissipates.

This approach is only possible when the board and staff create and advance a mission that describes both why and what. A different language emerges, enabling people to speak about opportunities to invest in programs that are making a huge difference in the community. Board and staff can focus on results, impact, and success. Organizations no longer need to project an image of being poor and needy. Instead, they can portray themselves as powerful partners with the community in meeting the needs of the homeless and hungry, providing education and spiritual services for children and adults, or meeting the health needs of its citizens. With this shift, donors become donor-investors.

PITFALL

The "tin-cup" approach to fundraising emphasizes the need to solicit money, not the mission or the relationships with supporters. When mission isn't front and center in fundraising, board members often lack the inspiration and the motivation to succeed at this important job.

This change in language, attitude, and positioning increases the willingness of board members and other volunteers to develop the relationships around shared values that lead to significant investment — and then to keep those individuals involved as donor-investors. The whole process of donor development takes on a new dimension. Rather than rushing into the solicitation, board members understand the importance of taking the time to develop a values-based and issues-focused relationship with a potential donor.

TIP

Cultivation activities include exposure to programs, impact, and people who have benefited, as well as those who provide programs for community benefit. The focus is on uncovering shared values and building a long-term relationship, not just on asking for money. Most important, a commitment to transformation replaces an emphasis on the transaction.

Mission then manifests itself again and again in the stewardship required to keep the transformational relationship strong — yet another way for board members to reinforce their own sense of mission while engaging others. You cannot have meaningful stewardship without a strong sense of mission. The board members who become involved in nurturing donor-investors should have the strongest sense of mission and of the way in which your organization is implementing it in the community. They will be able to tell the stories that keep the donor feeling as though the return on investment is very high.

QUESTIONS THE BOARD SHOULD ASK

1. Does our mission statement appear on our organization's Web site and in all electronic and print materials?

2. Do we link our mission directly to strategic planning and measure strategic goals and objectives against our mission?

3. Does every board and staff member have an "elevator speech" and an "elevator question" that deliver a succinct message about our organization?

4. Do we use a mission-driven approach to fundraising, focusing on how our organization meets needs in the community?

4

CHAPTER 4

USING MISSION TO POWER BOARD EFFECTIVENESS

The involvement of mission in effective board recruitment, orientation, and retention bridges the external and internal impact of mission.

RECRUITMENT

Too often, board recruitment is a random process — done at the last minute without a strategy. But recruitment becomes strategic when board members understand and embrace the mission.

Because values are at the heart of the mission, a primary criterion for selecting new board members is shared values. While organizations still look for board members with a complementary array of skills (such as problem solving, team building, or advocacy) and experience (such as fundraising, investments, or strategic communications), awareness of the mission dimension in board recruitment grows stronger. During board recruitment, just as during the cultivation of potential donors, there is greater focus on uncovering shared values through exposure to programs and people that embody those values.

In a professional association, members often see board service as a special asset on their resume. Certainly, members can hone their leadership skills by serving on the board or a committee, but the association must attract individuals who are familiar with the industry and also understand the needs of the membership at large. These board members consider their association as the spokesperson for all members and an instigator for improving the legal and political aspects of their professional environment. All association board members need to stand behind the mission that serves the entire membership.

Here are some tips for a mission-guided recruitment process:

Create a board profile to ensure strategic enlistment.
Develop a recruitment matrix based on the strategic plan, which incorporates the vision and is guided by the mission. Profile current board members' skills, work and board experience, demographic information, and community connections to assess what's needed in new board recruits. Include personal qualities in the matrix: board experience, group decision-making skills, strategic thinking ability, and interpersonal skills. Include less tangible qualities in the profile, too: For example, if the strategic plan calls for studying and improving the staff salary and benefits structure, consider recruiting a board member who has experience in human resources. Or if the board wants to improve its capacity for inquiry and strategic thinking, people who have served on boards worth emulating for their culture will be helpful.

Listen for shared values when making the initial contact with potential board members. Ask open-ended questions that encourage them to share their values and experiences. Even if the reason for their recruitment may initially be their financial, marketing, or other skills, be sure that their passion and interests align with your mission. Otherwise, board service would be frustrating for them and for the rest of the board.

Emphasize mutual agreement on mission as a qualification for board service. Let prospects know what the organization's mission is, why this meets an important need in the community, how the organization is meeting that need, and the match you see between your organization's mission and values and what the person believes and has experienced.

Help prospects learn more about the mission. Introduce them to board and staff members who can further explain and demonstrate the mission and its impact, and gauge the response of potential board members. Describe board member responsibilities, including keeping a focus on mission and what that means in your organization. One organization requires all interested board candidates to serve a year on a committee before they join the board. This ensures few "mission misfits" end up on the board.

TIP

Post your mission statement in the lobby of your organization, to greet everyone who enters. Frame it and place it on the wall or on the receptionist's desk; for board meetings, place it at every member's seat for quick reference during deliberations. For example, some organizations have printed the mission on the back of name cards or on paper placements that go in front of every board member. Others have placed the mission prominently on the wall in the room where board members regularly meet.

ORIENTATION

There are few better investments of time and money than a solid, formal, and rigorous board orientation. And there are few better platforms for ensuring that board members understand and have ownership of the mission.

An orientation should be equal parts information, inspiration, and motivation. Among the desired outcomes is an immediately higher level of comfort with mission advocacy. When contrasted with "orientation" that consists of handing new board members a binder and then asking if anyone has questions, the difference is profound. An early immersion in the mission and stories, an emphasis on impact, and an introduction to how board members can get involved start off the whole board experience positively. And the mission is the engine.

Here's how an orientation can be the perfect follow-up to a mission-guided recruitment process:

Share information and experiences that demonstrate impact. Invite program staff and service recipients to describe their work and relate their experiences. Accompany these program presentations with hard facts: number served, number still to be served, cost of service, funding sources, and so forth.

Inspire new board members with stories of involvement. Let new board members hear from people who have benefited from programs, as well as from other board members or volunteers who can speak with passion about their involvement and what it has meant in their lives. Inspiration also comes from a spirited discussion of the values that drive the mission and the organization.

Provide tools for motivation and engagement. At the end of the orientation, ask new board members to fill out a simple checklist of ways they would like to be involved. Give them the option to list any unique role or service they can provide. The checklists will serve as indicators of individual motivation, giving board and staff leadership the tools to shape a meaningful and productive mission-based role for the new member.

PITFALL

When "orientation" consists of handing new board members a binder and asking if they have questions about the organization, you're sending the wrong message about board service. If mission doesn't click from the start, you'll risk having bored, disengaged board members who don't know how to contribute.

BOARD MEMBER ENGAGEMENT AND RETENTION

Premature turnover on a board is often a sign of mission drift. People who come onto a board because they are passionate about the mission become disengaged when they feel that the mission is being overwhelmed by politics, trivia, poorly managed meetings, lack of focus, and wasted time. To retain excellent people, nonprofits need to continue focusing on the mission and the way in which it drives decisions and emphasis.

Here are some ideas for sustaining interest and engagement.

Improve board meetings. Board meetings are a key culprit in board member disaffection. Are your board meetings more like "bored" meetings? Do you have mission moments? Are you respectful of people's time and motivation? Have you rethought your board meetings as a platform for advancing the mission rather than getting mired in tedious and repetitive discussions about things that would be handled better by a committee?

Promote strategic thinking. Disconnection from the organization, and a subsequent inability to advance or keep the mission, is usually not the fault of the board member. It is most often the result of a board experience that was not motivating. Move away from meetings dominated by reports, inflexible agendas with too many items, and the tendency to rubber-stamp decisions. Promote exploration of questions that are meaningful to mission, give board members the information they need to stay current on internal and external strategic issues, and promote open, candid discussion.

Keep board members connected to mission. If you have diligently brought in board members whose values are consistent with those of the organization, you'll want to sustain their interest. You know they're dedicated to the mission, so channel their enthusiasm into areas where they can make a difference. Make appropriate committee and task force assignments. Arrange periodic "field trips" for board members to observe programs in action. Share news and information about your organization's field or service area. Plan an annual board retreat with substantive, mission-related content and opportunities for deep discussion. Encourage attendance at regional or national meetings of similar service providers that inspire board members to see the larger mission.

MISSION AND BOARD LEADERSHIP

Organizational advancement is predicated on clarity of mission; commitment to its implementation; and a continuing understanding that the mission reflects the shared values of the board, the staff, and the community. Nowhere should this be more evident than in board leadership.

While the election of a board chair is not often a hard-fought contest, it would be wonderful if the idea of board leadership were so enticing that more than one candidate wanted the job. One way to make it more attractive is to shift the primary responsibility of the chair from administrivia to mission. Mission advocacy can stimulate a continuous stream of willing leaders. When mission advocacy becomes the main task of board leadership, other organizational issues easily fall into place.

To build mission-inspired leadership, provide opportunities for people to engage in activities that will reinforce their own commitment to mission. For example, board members can share the mission with others by

- participating in board recruitment
- organizing and facilitating the board orientation
- mentoring new board members
- participating in donor or member cultivation activities
- serving as committee chairs
- participating in strategic planning
- participating in ongoing stewardships of donor-investors
- assisting with drafting or reviewing a new or revised mission statement

When an organization offers this kind of involvement, mission advancement becomes so internalized and natural that it no longer looms as a confusing part of the nonprofit board member's role. Instead, board members realize that what engages them is the mission, what keeps them is the mission, and what encourages them to get others involved is the match between their values and the mission. Their new understanding of the organization's mission and importance in the community frames and powers their leadership in membership, fundraising, marketing, advocacy, governance, board recruitment, board orientation, and tough decision making.

For more information on identification, recruitment, orientation, and development of board leaders, see *Structures and Practices of Nonprofit Boards,* Book 6 in the BoardSource Governance Series.

QUESTIONS THE BOARD SHOULD ASK

1. Do board candidates and new recruits know the mission and vision of our organization?

2. Does our board have a sense of shared values?

3. Does our board orientation use mission and vision to help educate, inspire, and motivate new board members?

4. Do we encourage veteran board members to participate in orientation as a "mission refresher"?

5. Do we use mission moments to continually motivate and inspire board members?

5

CHAPTER 5

STRATEGIC PLANNING: WHAT IT IS AND WHY YOU SHOULD DO IT

Mission has a pivotal place in strategic planning, the process that seeks the strategic fit between the mission of an organization and its internal strengths and external opportunities. Strategic planning develops a shared dream among the stakeholders of an organization and produces a blueprint for how to achieve that dream.

The strategic planning process is the perfect time for board members to consider their dreams and visions for an organization and to articulate the essence of its values. It gives board members the time and authorization to visualize, ponder, and debate the future within the context of known realities and facts. As Doug Eadie observes in *Boards That Work: A Practical Guide to Building Effective Association Boards,* "Planning surely has no peer as a vehicle for a board's exercise of creative, foresightful leadership" (ASAE, 1995).

So why does strategic planning sometimes conjure up at worst a sense of fear and at best a feeling of ambivalence, instead of those heady dreams and visions? Strategic planning experiences too often become bogged down in an endless cycle of meetings, sabotaged by outspoken naysayers or derailed by leaders uncommitted to the process and its results. Any potential to truly scrutinize the mission and envision the possibilities is squashed at the door.

Visioning fits into planning because strategic planning incorporates a change model — and change can be an intrinsic trait of an organization's vision. An organization that conducts strategic planning must be willing to change direction if necessary and imagine what that direction might look like.

A drug and alcohol day treatment program for teens, called Prism, was housed in the basement of a local church to which the program participants came each day before and after school. The organization had dreams of getting its own building and starting a charter school to gain private spaces for counseling as well as to provide a general education component so that participants could stay at one facility all day long. Strategic planning helped this small community-based organization articulate its vision and develop concrete goals and strategies that helped it obtain a significant grant for those purposes.

Your organization may not need to bring about dramatic change with every strategic plan. But strategic planning requires you to scrutinize all aspects of operations, recognize sacred items up front, and map out a course for the future.

STRATEGIC THINKING VS. STRATEGIC PLANNING

Boards that make mission-driven planning a part of their ongoing work are engaging in strategic thinking — a rewarding, productive way of doing the board's business that ultimately informs and supports strategic planning. *The Source: Twelve Principles That Power Exceptional Boards* (BoardSource, 2005) explains the difference:

- *Strategic planning:* In partnership with staff, boards draw on an understanding of organizational strengths and weaknesses, industry trends, and peer benchmarking to articulate priorities and monitor progress against financial and programmatic goals. After translating strategic priorities into action plans, they use these plans to assess the chief executive, drive meeting agendas, and shape board recruitment.

- *Strategic thinking:* Boards make strategic thinking part of regular, ongoing board work — not just part of an annual planning process. They ask far-ranging questions to help clarify thorny problems, offer breakthrough insights on pressing issues, present new ways of thinking about challenges and opportunities, and actively generate important strategic ideas.

As an integral part of board process, strategic thinking ultimately provides the rich, high-quality content for the strategic plan.

PITFALL

Planning is always difficult to fit in the middle of handling daily tasks, so a mere verbal agreement will not guarantee that planning will actually happen. To ensure the effort becomes more than a promise on paper only, obtain a firm commitment from all the key participants and budget specifically for strategic planning activities.

NATURE OF STRATEGIC PLANNING

Strategic planning is an organizational, political, and rational process: It examines all aspects of an organization, involves key internal and external stakeholders, and requires a certain level of logic and discipline. Although strategic planning incorporates a rational approach and requires analysis and critical thinking from its participants, creativity is also important. Creativity not only keeps the process interesting but also helps an organization envision the possibilities for itself. Remember, strategic planning is a sanctioned time for envisioning the future!

Yet like the progression of a dream or the creation of a work of art, strategic planning is a process and not an end unto itself. Just completing a strategic planning process does not make a plan. An organization must be vigilant about keeping intact the balance between process and product. Generations United — a national membership organization dedicated to improving the lives of children, youth, and older people through intergenerational strategies, programs, and public policies — activated its strategic plan to drive its work. Its success in meeting its goals, including greater attention from the media and public officials for intergenerational issues, shows how well this small organization has built on its strategic plan.

Strategic planning must fit into an organization's culture. What's important to your organization? What are its environment and atmosphere like? How often does the board usually meet? These are important elements to consider when developing the planning process and determining how to accomplish the work of planning. (For more about different approaches to strategic planning, see Chapter 6.)

WHY STRATEGIC PLANNING IS IMPORTANT

Strategic planning requires a deep and strong commitment from the leadership of an organization. The board must give a clear mandate to embark on a planning process, including an understanding of why it is planning now and what it hopes to achieve through the process. That mind-set must also be communicated widely, because successful strategic planning seeks ownership at every level of the organization.

In *Driving Strategic Planning: A Nonprofit Executive's Guide* (BoardSource, 2003), Deborah L. Kocsis and Susan A. Waechter articulate the benefits of the board's involvement:

> With the board grounded in the rationale and choices underlying the organization's long-term strategy, it is better able to govern. The strategic plan will eventually guide the board in future decision making; it will facilitate and inspire the board's fundraising efforts; it will help the board better understand how the organization operates.

Because a board must be clear about its motivation for embarking on strategic planning, it might be useful to look at some reasons why strategic planning is important. Organizations conduct strategic planning to

- clarify the mission to all stakeholders

- assess, reassess, and adjust programs

- reaffirm that an organization is headed where it wants to go or should be going

- focus thinking outside the box

- develop a framework within which to make difficult programmatic and financial decisions

- address external uncertainties and change

- garner financial support (particularly from funders who require a strategic plan)

- build teamwork, communication, and expertise among board and staff
- measure organizational effectiveness by incorporating evaluation into the process

BUILDING EVALUATION INTO THE STRATEGIC PLAN

Strategic planning allows the board to measure whether (or the extent to which) the organization has been effective in accomplishing its mission. It offers a road map and benchmarks to measure organizational effectiveness because the measurements identified through strategic planning are key indicators of performance.

Many organizations include performance measures or evaluative components in their strategic plans to enhance the ability to successfully implement the plan. Performance measures for each strategic goal and the associated objectives (see Chapter 7) define what success would look like if these goals and objectives were achieved.

For example, if XYZ Organization has a strategic goal to increase its visibility and an objective to develop new partnerships with government, educational, and community organizations, XYZ should determine how many new partnerships it seeks to develop and what evidence or outcomes will indicate an impact on the organization's visibility. Some organizations make the development of an evaluation plan an objective within the strategic plan.

STRATEGIC PLANNING ROLES

Strategic planning is a group effort that benefits from teamwork among the board, the chief executive, and the staff.

- The board works in close partnership with the chief executive but must own the results of the process. Organizing the details of the process is up to the staff, but each board member should contribute to the strategy development and understanding of the consequences of board decisions. Before the planning process starts, the board must choose the right approach to fit the organization's phase in life and determine the feasibility of planning at that moment.

- The chief executive manages the strategic planning process. The chief executive is often the visionary, articulating the ideas for the future and then seeking the board's blessing. The chief executive usually instigates the idea of planning and then oversees the execution of the plan. In addition to coordinating the participation of needed collaborators, the chief executive may delegate some of the individual tasks to board or staff while ensuring that planning proceeds as expected.

- The staff members provide relevant context to planning because they are so close to the everyday workings of the organization. They are often tasked with researching the organization's external and internal factors and organizing meetings and retreats to bring all the players together. After the overall plan is defined, the staff drafts the operational plans for implementation — the next step to the strategic plan. Ultimately, the staff translates the board-approved strategic plan into workable directives and timelines.

TIMEFRAME

Strategic plans typically cover periods of two to five years, so strategic planning occurs in similar time intervals. Other kinds of plans (see Chapter 6) encompass shorter or longer periods of time and are often the result of, or incorporated into, strategic plans. The frequency of strategic planning, however, should not be decided arbitrarily. It depends on the environment, what's in the plan, and how long your organization needs to accomplish its goals and objectives.

Whether the plan covers two, three, or five years, it should be reviewed and, if necessary, updated annually through operational, action, or tactical plans (see Chapter 6). The following circumstances may prompt planning outside the two- to five-year framework:

- The goals and objectives from a previous plan have been accomplished ahead of schedule.

- A significant change in leadership occurs (the chief executive or the board leadership).

- The organization's financial situation changes dramatically due to unanticipated changes in the external environment, such as an unexpected large bequest or the loss of a major grant or funding source.

- The organization's reputation is affected by a scandal — brought about by fiscal mismanagement or insufficient board oversight, for instance — and it needs to restore credibility and move forward.

WHEN TO POSTPONE STRATEGIC PLANNING

The board and staff leadership must carefully consider their readiness to conduct strategic planning before embarking on the process. You'll know that the time is not right if you observe the following signs:

- The time and financial resources needed will jeopardize the financial stability of the organization.

- Leadership (board or staff) has not invested time in planning to plan.

- Turmoil or conflict exists among board members or between board and staff.

- A significant change in leadership just occurred (unless the new leadership seeks direction from a strategic plan to chart a new course for the organization).

- The process and plan will create unrealistic expectations.

- The organization is experiencing a crisis.

- There is a lack of organizational knowledge of strategic planning or a deficit of strategic thinking. (Organizations can, however, learn strategic thinking from the planning process, and outside consultants can help with the knowledge.)

- Sufficient information about the external context for planning has not been obtained.

- The plan is unlikely to be implemented.

The board of a large, well-respected mental health organization launched strategic planning that was stymied by the removal of the chief executive after serious misconduct was revealed in the initial planning phases. In this case, the planning process unwittingly uncovered serious problems and planning was necessarily put on hold while the organization weathered its crisis.

Strategic planning at its core forces forward thinking, and not every board or organization is equipped to think and act this way. If there are barriers to strategic planning, the board must find remedies to them. Organizational readiness for planning is a sign of organizational health, and strategic planning is a good entry point to the continuous cycle of planning and evaluation for strong, accountable organizations.

TIP

Be sure your organization is ready to embark on a strategic planning process. Reasons to postpone planning include internal conflict, insufficient information about the external context for planning, or a board not fully committed to the process.

USING CONSULTANTS

Many organizations hire an outside consultant to facilitate the strategic planning process, though one is not always necessary. A consultant provides overall expertise and is particularly helpful if an organization has little or no experience with strategic planning or had an unpleasant experience in the past. An outside consultant can

- design and guide a process that will work for a particular organization

- establish a schedule

- set agendas

- facilitate meetings and the planning process

- conduct environmental research

- craft questionnaires and conduct interviews for perceptual analysis

- provide neutrality for contentious issues and ensure they are addressed directly

Using a consultant also allows all stakeholders to participate freely. Board members and staff can muck around in the issues and voice an opinion without needing to maintain a neutral stance. A consultant can be a neutral third party, a resource, or even a "devil's advocate" to keep the conversation focused and productive.

Consultants, of course, cost money, and some funders offer technical assistance grants to help cover these kinds of expenses because they realize the value of effective planning for an organization. A board can find qualified consultants by asking other organizations or funders for recommendations or by checking with local professional associations or universities. Talking with other organizations can provide a wealth of information about consultants being considered to help design and facilitate a strategic planning process.

Charles Bruner offers some helpful questions to guide discussions with other organizations about consultants they have engaged (National Center for Service Integration, 1993):

- What was the nature and scope of the work done by the consultant?

- Did the consultant have an objective approach to the required work?

- Did the consultant demonstrate professional competence and integrity?

- How constructively did the consultant work with the organization's personnel?

- Was the work completed on schedule and at the quality level anticipated?

- Was the consultant able to communicate effectively with those involved in the consultation engagement?

- Were the consultant's recommendations practical and sufficient to the organization's needs?

- What is the overall evaluation as to the value of the consulting engagement?

- Would the organization use the consultant again if there were a need for this kind of professional service?

If a consultant is hired, a contract should outline expectations, deliverables, and a time frame to ensure that the work is completed as anticipated and on schedule.

? QUESTIONS THE BOARD SHOULD ASK

1. How often do we conduct strategic planning? Does that cycle make sense for the organization?

2. When we are ready to undertake a planning process, are we clear about why we are planning?

3. Are we clear about the roles of the board, chief executive, and staff in strategic planning? Do we honor the distinctions?

4. Have we used consultants in the most effective ways possible? If we have never used a consultant, should we consider doing so?

6

CHAPTER 6
APPROACHES TO STRATEGIC PLANNING

Board members may have encountered many different types of plans and planning processes in the business, public, and nonprofit sectors. Experience in planning is important for board members to share. It is also helpful for board members to understand what kinds of plans are most common in nonprofit organizations, which ones are most successful for what situations, and why plans are essential to successful management strategies.

Much of the real value of planning lies in the process. Stronger and deeper relationships and communication patterns develop among the board, stakeholders, and staff. The learning and experience that accumulate as planning progresses enhance individual board service and boost the effectiveness of the board as a whole. The new perspectives that emerge from planning yield a deeper understanding of the organization's mission and potential. Each time an organization goes through a strategic planning cycle, it gains much more than a written document.

When choosing a planning approach, each organization needs to reflect on what's appropriate at this moment in its life cycle. What worked five or 10 years ago may not work today. This chapter describes a selection of approaches for organizations to consider. If you are new to planning, you might start with a mission focus and assess the external and internal circumstances that affect your future. If you have a history of strategic planning, you may choose to look only at critical issues. Or you may simply brainstorm scenarios that demand your attention so that you're prepared for the unexpected.

TERMS DEFINED

The semantics of planning (and evaluation) can put off even the most well-intentioned staff and board members. After all, what really is the difference between long-range plans, strategic plans, and operational plans? And isn't a business plan just the same as any of these other plans?

The following terms may be used differently and have different meanings in the public and private sectors — and may even be used interchangeably in the nonprofit vernacular — but they are distinct.

A long-range plan, outlining a long-term (10 to 20 years) vision and direction, includes operating assumptions based upon a relatively stable external environment. A long-range plan is useful when an organization does not anticipate change down the road. It emphasizes a vision and long-term direction more than specific annual objectives.

A long-range plan differs from a strategic plan in that the latter assumes an organization should constantly monitor changes in the external environment and respond accordingly through more frequent planning cycles. A long-range plan is developed and used by the board and staff.

A strategic plan defines what an organization should do within the near (two to five years) future, why, and how. Strategic planning assumes nonprofit organizations operate in a constantly changing environment that must be monitored and adjusted to in terms of strategic directions and activities. A strategic plan — which usually encompasses broad strategic goals and strategies but not specific action steps — is developed and used primarily by the board, staff, and other key stakeholders.

An operational plan, also known as an action plan or tactical plan, converts the strategic goals and objectives in a strategic plan into annual plans. An operational plan incorporates the strategic goals and their related objectives and strategies and identifies specific action steps, timelines, budget requirements, responsible people or organizational area, and a monitoring and evaluation process. Although the board of directors approves and monitors an operational plan, staff and volunteers most frequently develop, implement, and evaluate the plan.

A business plan may be developed for the whole organization or for specific programs. It specifies the purpose and provides a snapshot of the market, clients, competition, finances, and key personnel for accomplishing the stated purpose within a given time frame. A business plan includes elements of the strategic plan and operational plan, particularly in the strategic areas of marketing and financial management. It is often used in developing a new program or generating earned income through some mission-related business venture.

In some respects, a business plan is similar to a funding proposal. Like an operational plan, a business plan may be approved and monitored by the board of directors, but its development, implementation, and evaluation are the primary responsibilities of the staff and, in some instances, selected volunteers.

Nonprofit organizations use many other kinds of plans to guide the work of separate functional areas such as program, human resources, finance, marketing, and fundraising. These plans are the responsibility of the chief executive and other staff, not the board. The board needs to ensure that such plans are in place and monitored, perhaps with some oversight by the related board committees.

COMMON STRATEGIC PLANNING METHODS

Organizations embarking on strategic planning for the first time — or after a long absence — will probably find it most beneficial to follow the traditional planning process, which includes these steps:

- **Plan to plan.** Typically, the chief executive takes the lead in preparing the organization for strategic planning. This step includes identifying a time frame, establishing a budget, determining who will participate (for example, board members, donors, and constituents), and clarifying what form the final plan will take.

- **Undertake a SWOT analysis.** Board members not only identify the organization's strengths, weaknesses, opportunities, and threats but also discuss potential strategic responses.

- **Review the mission.** Revisit why the organization exists and the unique role it plays within the local, national, or global community.

- **Generate strategies, goals, and objectives.** These should be viewed within the context of the mission, so all of the organization's undertakings ultimately contribute to advancing its mission.

- **Monitor the plan.** Identify specific data the board can use to review progress toward the anticipated outcomes and, when necessary, make adjustments to the plan.

For organizations that are ready to define and focus on larger issues, or those experienced with strategic planning, experts recommend that the approach suit the organization's individual circumstances. Nonprofit strategic planning literature offers a variety of options. Three possible methods are the critical issues approach, the management goals approach, and the scenario approach.

The critical issues approach, used often in nonprofit organizations, offers a bottom-up, inclusive planning process that focuses on the organization's current context. It works well for organizations that have conducted strategic planning before and are looking to fine-tune their goals and strategies in response to new developments and changes in their external environment. These organizations may want to improve management capacity or mission implementation, but they may not want to implement any dramatically new ways of doing business.

In this planning approach, goals and strategies emerge relatively easily from the critical issues identified, and organizations may find implementing a plan rather straightforward. The board is involved in this type of planning every step of the way. Board members participate on the planning committee and have a hand in deliberating the critical issues and developing the subsequent goals and strategies.

DECIDING ON THE DETAILS

With leadership from the chief executive, the committee or group overseeing the strategic planning process should begin by answering three essential questions:

1. Why does the organization want to do strategic planning?

2. Is the organization ready to do strategic planning?

3. What are some of the strategic issues that are likely to surface during the process?

The next set of questions helps the group outline the steps and logistics of the process:

1. Who chairs the strategic planning committee?
   Usually a board member

2. Who are the organizations' key stakeholders?
   Board members, staff, clients, volunteers, funders

3. Which stakeholders will be on the planning committee?
   Board members and usually representatives from all stakeholder groups

4. How will other stakeholders be engaged?
   Surveys, individual interviews, focus groups

5. What analytic work will be completed?
   Perceptual analysis, mandate analysis, environmental scanning, (see page 70-71 for definitions.)

6. What specific steps will occur, and what is the timetable?
   Meetings and retreats to provide strategic direction, including developing or reviewing mission, vision, values, goals, and objectives

7. Who will staff the process?
   Staff members to coordinate meetings, schedules, logistics, and communication

8. Will an outside consultant be engaged and to do what?
   External consultant to facilitate the entire process or to serve as content consultant, provide expertise in developing goals and objectives, and help the organization research its external environment

The management goals approach is similar to traditional corporate, top-down planning. This option assumes that the leadership of an organization is in the best position to think strategically about its future and to formulate the key goals necessary to realize that future.

With this approach, a small group of board and staff leaders articulates a set of management goals and then engages other board members, staff, and stakeholders in developing strategies to achieve these goals. The board is involved as part of the leadership team, but it may rely primarily on the perspectives and goals of the chief executive to guide the planning process and shape the plan's contents. Because this approach is less inclusive, the board may not be as involved as in some of the other options.

The scenario approach offers various scenarios or pictures of what the future of an organization might look like. It presents different options in narrative or story form, challenging participants to see the possibilities in concrete terms instead of imagining them in the abstract. Sometimes the alternatives include best-case, worst-case, and middle-of-the-road options.

Bryan Barry, in *Strategic Planning Workbook for Nonprofit Organizations* (Fieldstone Alliance, 2001), says this approach may be useful for new or young organizations that have never conducted planning because it stimulates big-picture thinking and helps participants envision significant shifts in direction. It may also work for organizations that need to revise their missions or develop new programs and services to serve their constituencies. With the scenario approach, however, some organizations may find it difficult to figure out how to move from the big picture to the implementation steps needed.

The board may be involved in scenario planning by participating on the committee that helps craft the various scenarios and/or by voting on the options offered. The board may also help the staff develop goals and strategies for the strategic plan that will support the chosen scenario.

It's perfectly acceptable to modify one of these (or other) planning methods to accommodate an organization's needs and its planning parameters. A strategic planning process must fit the culture of your organization, its leadership style, and the results you hope to achieve. You don't have to choose the same approach each time the planning cycle comes around. Indeed, a mixture of approaches over time may encourage innovation, critical thinking, and eventually better results for the organization and its quest to attain its mission.

☛ TIP

Don't automatically adopt a traditional planning method. During the planning-to-plan phase, assess carefully how thorough a process you need. You may not need to revamp the entire plan, but you may need to re-identify, refocus, or redefine your main critical issues.

HOW TO GET STARTED

To help you get the ball rolling with strategic planning, we offer this example using the critical issues model. Nonprofit organizations often use this planning method when they do not need to engage in a full-scale strategic planning process but when timing or circumstances indicate that it's necessary to identify the critical issues affecting the organization and its future. The critical issues model is effective because it

- reaches out to all stakeholders in an inclusive process

- emphasizes a partnership between the board and staff

- follows straightforward and rational steps

- forms a continuous cycle with evaluation

The board is involved in each phase of this strategic planning process through hands-on involvement on the planning committee or task force or through communication about this group's progress. The committee reports to and is accountable to the board. Often the chair of the board leads the committee or task force or is at least one of its members.

Staff members are responsible for coordinating the logistics of the planning process and are engaged as active participants. They are most familiar with the intricacies of the programmatic and functional areas of the organization. They too, play a key role in shaping a plan that will ultimately be theirs to implement.

The board may initiate and conduct the strategic planning process, but the chief executive and staff members usually drive the process.

The critical issues model has three phases:

PHASE 1: PLANNING TO PLAN

This phase focuses on what the planning process will look like and who will be involved. Board members and the chief executive are important decision makers at this stage. The board chair or the board planning committee chair (usually a board member but not necessarily the chair), along with the chief executive, convene a small group of board and staff members for one or two meetings.

PHASE 2: INFORMATION GATHERING AND ANALYSIS

The information-gathering and analysis (analytic) phase examines the organization's internal and external environments and surveys its stakeholders. This phase is all about research and data gathering and assessing the data within the context of strategic planning. The board designates a group of people or task force to identify, collect, and interpret the relevant data sources. While the nature and scope of the work will dictate the time required, many organizations allow about three months.

This phase might include the following research and evaluation activities:

Perceptual analysis — evaluating stakeholders' views of the organization and the issues it faces. A stakeholder survey might include some of these questions:

- How would you rate the organization's programs and services?

- How would you rate the overall quality of interaction between staff and clientele?

- How would you rate the organization's fundraising efforts?

- How would you rate the organization's overall image?

- To what extent is the public aware of the organization?

- What is the organization's greatest strength and greatest weakness?

- What are the most critical challenges facing the organization?

The entire board is also surveyed or interviewed during this phase, giving each member the opportunity to contribute directly to issues identification.

Mandate analysis — looking at all of the legal or binding documents such as the bylaws, incorporation requirements, funding contingencies, certifications, and other organizational commitments that must be considered during the planning process. A few board members may be involved in looking at legal documents or donor commitments.

Environmental scan — determining elements of the external world and the internal context that affect the organization and its mission and operations. In the external scan, trends are identified within specific categories, including social and demographic, political and legal, economic, technology, volunteerism, fundraising, and the subsector or mission focus of the organizations (such as health care, the arts, education, or housing). In the internal scan, it's important to look at objective elements, such as organization charts and policies and procedures, as well as subjective elements, such as organizational culture and decision-making styles. Some board members can assist in analyzing the implications of the external and internal contexts for the organization and identifying potential ways to address these implications during the planning process.

Some nonprofit organizations conduct a limited competitive analysis of the products and services that other organizations provide within a particular subsector. The purpose of this analysis is to determine how the organization compares with its peers on key operational factors, such as clientele demographics, product features, office hours, product placement, and pricing. Given the multi-product nature of many nonprofits, difficulty in collecting comparative data, and the costs associated with this type of analysis, many organizations do not conduct a comprehensive competitive analysis.

PITFALL

No matter which strategic planning method you choose, if you don't incorporate a mission discussion into the process, you may veer off course and get carried away by new, exciting endeavors.

PHASE 3: COMMITTEE DELIBERATION

In this phase the planning committee pulls together the information gathered during the second phase and systematically recommends any modifications to the mission, reaffirms or develops the vision and values, identifies the critical issues, and fashions the goals and objectives that will be contained in the strategic plan. Many organizations allow approximately four to five months to complete this phase.

The SWOT (strengths, weaknesses, opportunities, threats) analysis undertaken during this phase allows the planning committee to examine carefully an organization's advantages and disadvantages. The committee considers specific data on programs and services, finances, membership, marketing, human resources, and other areas of the organization gathered from ongoing evaluation efforts — another link between planning and evaluation.

Board members who don't serve on the planning committee are frequently asked to participate in some of these activities. They may be asked to contribute input on the mission, vision, and values statements; to join in the critical issues discussion; or to help form the goals and objectives. The key stages of the committee deliberation phase include

- developing or reviewing mission, vision, and values statements

- conducting a SWOT analysis

- identifying and prioritizing critical issues

- developing goals and strategies to address critical issues

- drafting a strategic plan

- refining and finalizing the plan

- presenting the plan to the board for deliberation and approval

Organizations structure their planning meetings in different ways depending on their culture. Some hold a series of two- or three-hour meetings (usually during the early mornings or evenings), while others have one or more retreats (partial- or full-day) to work through the process. Other organizations use a combination.

NEXT STEPS

Following the three planning phases, the full board reviews and discusses the strategic plan and any revisions to the organization's mission and then votes on acceptance. As implementation of the plan begins, an evaluation process is also set in motion to regularly assess performance.

FINDING THE RIGHT PLANNING METHODS

A customized strategic planning process helped the National Human Services Assembly — an association of leading national nonprofits in the fields of health, human and community development, and human services — focus on a small set of big-picture issues. The staff and board had struggled with the balance between providing membership service and meeting human needs. As a result, says president and CEO Irv Katz, "we were several inches deep on a couple of topics and a sixteenth of an inch deep on many others."

Instead of applying a single strategic planning model, the organization combined several approaches. Starting with a traditional "environmental scan-to-plan" process, the organization added ideas from Jim Collins' monograph *Good to Great and the Social Sectors*. Then, because there were some major unknowns in the Assembly's environment, they incorporated elements of scenario planning. Katz says this planning process "enabled us to establish where we are on the service-to-collective action continuum" and create three central issue areas. There's a clearer understanding about mission and critical issues and about the balance of purpose that had been such a struggle for staff and board. "What we do is clearly driven by this understanding."

CONTENTS OF A STRATEGIC PLAN

By the time a strategic plan gets to the board for formal approval, there should be no surprises. The plan articulates the collective thinking about the organization at a given point in time based on the circumstances in which the organization finds itself. It should be clear and logical in addressing critical issues and setting up the necessary goals and objectives that will guide the board and staff. Board and staff members should see and celebrate their handiwork in the plan itself.

Strategic plans usually contain the following elements:

Mission, vision, and core values statements — These express the organization's reason for being, articulate its ideal or preferred future and that of the community it serves, and identify the values that serve as timeless guiding principles for those most closely associated with the organization. (For more about how to develop these key statements, which are the foundation for strategic planning, see Chapters 1 and 2.)

Strategic goals — These define the outcomes the organization would like to achieve in response to critical issues or fundamental challenges. Consider these questions when developing strategic goals:

- What critical, strategic issue does this goal address?

- What are the consequences of not addressing this issue?

- How does this goal help the organization fulfill its mission?

- Does the goal build on organizational strength or address an organizational weakness?

Objectives — These state the end results that will support the achievement of the strategic goals. They indicate what the organization is striving for and provide the link between goals and performance measures. Objectives should be measurable (responsibility, timeframe, outcome) and are often distinct. Consider these questions when developing objectives:

- What are the practical options or choices the organization might pursue to address this issue and achieve the goal?

- What are the barriers to realizing these options?

Some organizations might use strategies instead of objectives in their strategic plans. In this context, strategies define the actions, directions, or means to the end that the organization will pursue to achieve its strategic goals. Strategies indicate how the organization will spend its time and allocate its resources. Organizations also describe tactics — the programs, services, or activities that the staff designs to achieve strategies or objectives. Tactics are part of the operational plan, not the strategic plan.

Performance measures — These provide evidence of the inputs (resources such as people, money, and materials), outputs (services provided), and outcomes (desired results). Many strategic plans do not include performance measures as part of the plan; rather, such measures are incorporated into the operational (tactical, action) plan or individual program plans. However, the following questions may be useful during planning and while developing a performance measurement strategy:

- How does the organization define success for itself? What does the outcome or the impact look like?

- Does the organization have a method for documenting and analyzing various performance measures?

- Does the staff build evaluation plans into program and action plans?

In the end, a strategic plan should be a succinct document that is not too long; easy to read; and clearly sets forth the mission, vision, strategic goals, and objectives of an organization for the near future. Most strategic plans have about three to five key strategic goals, though some may have more. Most strategic plans also include an introductory section (which provides a brief history of the organization and factors that led to strategic planning), an overview of the planning process, a conclusion, and a list of the strategic planning committee or task force members.

QUESTIONS THE BOARD SHOULD ASK

1. Have we considered all the options and chosen a planning method that works best for the organization? Are we flexible enough to combine approaches if that suits our culture?

2. How do we invite board members who are not on the planning committee to participate in the process?

3. Do we include performance measures in our strategic plan?

4. How do we keep our strategic plan active and visible within and outside the organization?

CHAPTER 7

EVALUATION: WHAT IT IS AND WHY YOU SHOULD DO IT

Evaluation, at a basic level, is figuring out something's value or worth by looking at it carefully. The term suggests a subjective process. But evaluation that is implemented systematically helps an organization move beyond subjectivity and introduces a level of objectivity to important management decisions.

In *Learning as We Go,* a briefing paper, Peter J. York advocates a view of evaluation that emphasizes internal learning. When organizations conduct evaluation only to prove to others that they've done what they said they would do, they miss a significant opportunity to "strengthen programs and services, use resources more efficiently and effectively, and share models of success."

Successful planning depends on evaluation that is systematic, ongoing, and focused on programs and operations. Continuous evaluation, says York, gives leaders "an intuitive understanding... of their operations and programs" and provides the information necessary "to adequately assess how well [the] organization is adhering to its mission and achieving the desired impact." It's up to the board to ensure that the organization's intended results are not only achieved to a certain degree but also desired in the first place.

Evaluation is primarily a staff-implemented activity. The board's responsibility for evaluation should focus primarily on measuring organizational effectiveness, which is discussed in more detail in Chapter 9. In order to measure organizational effectiveness, however, an organization must implement evaluation plans that document and assess different components of an organization.

"Every good strategic plan should have outcome measures that can be tracked," says governance consultant Bob Andringa. The board should ask the chief executive for a schedule of reports that track the key outcomes noted in the plan. Then, there has to be a readiness and willingness to change the plan when it becomes clear that a new initiative is not working. And the planning process itself should be evaluated by board and staff together, so the next round will be more effective than the last.

The staff is responsible for evaluating an organization's core programs, as well as areas such as fundraising, finance, marketing, and human resources. The board should ensure that these kinds of assessments take place regularly, while respecting the clear boundaries between board and staff roles. For both board and staff, evaluation results provide a learning tool to gain a comprehensive view of whether the organization is effective at achieving its mission.

PETER DRUCKER ON SELF-ASSESSMENT

Peter Drucker, known as the "father of modern management," believed that effective and ethical management is the precursor to a healthy society. He advocated evaluation as the principal requirement of leadership because it equips boards to make all the important judgments that are so essential to effective governance and sound management. His widely adopted approach to self-assessment centers on five basic questions:

1. What is our mission?

2. Who is our customer?

3. What does the customer value?

4. What are the results?

5. What is our plan?

Source: Drucker Foundation Self-Assessment Tool: Participant Workbook (Peter F. Drucker Foundation for Nonprofit Management and Jossey-Bass, 1999)

TERMS DEFINED

Board members should understand these basic evaluation terms:

Social indicators — Data points or numerical measures that reflect the status of a problem or condition of a group of people before program implementation. Social indicators are used to help define specific needs (such as infant mortality rates, federal industry-related quality controls, or proficiency test scores), as well as the type of program activities that might address those needs.

Inputs — Resources used to produce the programs, services, or activities of an organization, such as people, money, equipment, and materials.

Outputs — Quantifiable products or services delivered and/or people served by an organization, such as number of houses, meals, classes, sessions, performances, and clients.

Outcomes — Desired results of a program on its participants, including benefits and changes in condition. Examples include increased number of bills passed after improvement of an association's lobbying efforts, decreased unemployment among welfare recipients who participated in a job-training program, or increased test scores from students who participated in a tutoring program.

Impacts — Longer-term behavioral results of programs. Impacts can be considered more global or community based than outcomes because impacts demonstrate changed behavior over the long term for a larger group of people. Outcomes can contribute to overall, larger impacts. Examples include a reduction in fatal accidents after successfully lobbying for regulation of air bags in cars, the continued full employment of job-training program participants over time, or improved high school graduation rates among students whose test scores increased following tutoring.

Indicators — Data points or numerical measures that reflect the level of achievement of an outcome at various stages. Outcome indicators (or just indicators) measure incremental change, such as number of clients who found employment after participating in a job-training program (intermediate indicator) and number and percentage of clients who found employment and were gainfully employed 18 months later (end indicator).

Dashboards — Brief reports of progress toward achieving outcomes. These at-a-glance status updates are usually provided in specified increments such as a week, month, quarter, or year. Dashboards are not an evaluation techniques but simply ways to visually display information or report intermediate indicators.

Benchmarks — Standards by which outcomes are measured, such as against best practices in a field or industry, by past performance levels of a particular program, or even against the mission of an organization itself. Benchmarks provide comparative information.

Outcomes measurement — Systematic data gathering and monitoring of intended consequences of a program or service. Outcomes measurement assesses the outcomes themselves to determine if the desired results have been achieved. It is often considered part of performance measurement and overall program evaluation.

Performance measurement — Systematic gathering and monitoring of inputs, outputs, and outcomes. Performance measurement includes outcomes measurement and refers to the regular reporting of all the performance information.

Program evaluation — Systematic process that gathers and assesses information about a program, including performance measures, program implementation, quality, and/or client satisfaction among other elements. Program evaluation includes performance and outcomes measurement and answers the why, how, and what questions about an organization's programs and services (see Chapter 8).

Organizational effectiveness evaluation — Process of documenting and analyzing program outcomes as well as other key organizational areas such as effectiveness of service coordination and implementation, financial stability, human resource capability, and visibility. Measuring organizational effectiveness includes program evaluation (see Chapter 9).

TIP

Always involve those who implement plans in defining evaluation measures for their programs and projects so that progress is reasonable as well as challenging.

WHEN TO DO EVALUATION

The timing and frequency of evaluation for organizational areas such as marketing and fundraising should correspond to the timeframe of the related plans. Evaluation is a goals-oriented process and can only document and measure the achievement of goals that were established during the most recent planning cycle.

For example, fundraising may be evaluated annually to correspond to an annual development plan. Or, a particular marketing effort could be evaluated over two to three years to correspond to a marketing initiative designated for that timeframe. Benchmarks or incremental indicators can give the board and staff periodic information about progress in certain organizational areas.

REWARDS AND PITFALLS OF EVALUATION

Evaluation plays an important part in understanding how an organization is doing and where it's headed. Here are a few of the many rewards of evaluation:

- An impartial assessment of activity compared to established goals gives the board and management tools to ensure that performance is optimal.

- Clients can benefit from programs that have been improved because of evaluation.

- External validation of programs can boost the morale of both board and staff.

- Information obtained from evaluation can support fundraising and marketing activities.

- Funders like to see effective evaluation strategies in place; they may be more inclined to support an organization that can demonstrate specific results, even if those results are not always positive.

- Accrediting bodies often require evaluation, particularly information from outcomes measurement.

Even though the rewards of evaluation far outweigh its potential pitfalls, it's helpful to be aware of some of the hazards and note briefly how they might be addressed.

 PITFALL

If you neglect the basics — stating deadlines, assigning responsibility — you have forgotten that accountability makes skillfully drafted measures actually happen.

CHALLENGE	ACTION
It may be difficult to convince already overworked staff to focus on evaluation activities.	Management should build evaluation activities into job descriptions to reassure staff members that their time spent on evaluation is expected and worthwhile.
In an effort to garner quantitative data, other important qualitative data sources and their related understandings can be overlooked.	Use both qualitative and quantitative measurement strategies to gather a variety of data.
Sometimes results, whether positive or negative, cannot be attributed directly to any cause or to any one cause.	Acknowledge tenuous cause-and-effect links and be able to build a case incrementally for results, again using many indicators and data sources.
Some outcomes take longer or are more difficult to measure than originally anticipated.	Build in the proper time needed for thorough evaluation (to be determined by the nature of the program or organizational area being evaluated) and share incremental results along the way.
Some boards have the potential to micromanage when it comes to evaluation.	Emphasize that implementing program evaluation is a staff responsibility — and ultimately a learning tool for both board and staff — with decisions about what, when, and how made at the staff level.
Figuring out the right questions to ask in the evaluation process can be daunting.	If an outside consultant is not available to help in this area, ask for feedback from funders or colleagues in the field.

? QUESTIONS THE BOARD SHOULD ASK

1. Have we made evaluation an intrinsic part of organizational culture?

2. Is there resistance to evaluation in our organization? Where and why? What can we do to change?

3. At the board level, do we discuss and implement the results of organizational evaluation?

4. In what ways has evaluation improved our organization?

CHAPTER 8
EVALUATING PROGRAMS

Program evaluation is a practical tool that an organization uses to track and assess what it does. It is essential to improving programs and services for constituents. While program evaluation designs may resemble some research designs, evaluation need not be considered theory-based academic research. Program evaluation is simply a learning tool for the board and management to help them make decisions about the future. Program evaluation also provides concrete evidence to support advocacy and fundraising efforts.

Systematic program evaluation that includes outcomes measurement takes the subjectivity out of justifying an organization's existence and introduces objectivity by enabling an organization to report valid results. Ultimately, program evaluation helps an organization and its board ensure the integrity of programming in pursuit of mission. Evaluation also helps staff and the board determine which programs remain valid because they are closely tied to fulfilling the mission and which programs exist simply because they have always been there.

Responsibility for program evaluation belongs primarily to the organization's program staff, with oversight from the chief executive or executive management. But commitment to program evaluation — particularly outcomes measurement — from the very top is essential. Board members should want outcomes-based program evaluation because it can yield the kinds of data that help the board make decisions about programs and resource allocation during strategic planning.

For the board, evaluation results contribute to the big-picture context that guides its decision making. Just as it does not manage programs, the board does not evaluate programs. The board has these four general responsibilities related to evaluation:

- advocating for program evaluation that includes outcomes and performance measurement

- ensuring that program evaluation is conducted

- supporting management's allocation of people and time to do evaluation

- reviewing periodic reports regarding outcomes and performance measurement

PITFALL

Giving highly detailed program reports to the board may invite micromanagement. Let the chief executive decide when it is time to highlight a program and provide a more comprehensive report that shows evolution and progress.

WHO IS INVOLVED

Program staff is most often responsible for program evaluation. Staff members are closest to a program and its activities, but their physical and emotional proximity may introduce a level of subjectivity that careful program evaluation seeks to diminish. Program staff could look for certain outcomes and not disclose others or discount unanticipated indicators.

To avoid the potential for, or even perception of, staff bias, an organization may consider bringing in an external evaluation consultant. Also, evaluation expertise may be necessary for particularly complex programs that have many different yet interrelated components, each with different anticipated outcomes and possible measurement methods.

An organization's clients or constituents are also important participants in program evaluation. They are the primary sources of data, and their behaviors and attitudes (outcomes) are often what an organization seeks to measure. When possible, an organization should be explicit when initiating a program regarding its expectations for program participants to participate in evaluation activities. By doing so, the organization diminishes the potential for reticence or suspicion from the people who hold the most valuable information about a program and its impact.

PROGRAM EVALUATION STRATEGIES

Comprehensive program evaluation has two components. Outcomes measurement determines how a program is working by demonstrating actual results. Performance measurement measures program inputs and outputs to determine the quality and effectiveness of program implementation. By measuring outcomes and implementation, an organization will get a better idea of total program performance.

Because the board is not involved in the detailed analysis of program outcomes, it needs to make sure it gets adequate information on the success of the overall program. The board should expect program evaluation to be based on qualitative and quantitative data gathered through a variety of methods, including surveys, interviews, focus groups, pre- and post-tests, observations, and assessments of products developed from program participation.

Many nonprofit organizations use a logic model as a framework for both planning their programs and evaluating how well those programs are (or aren't) working to achieve the desired outcomes. Because of its visual component, a logic model helps staff envision all the various components of a program and how they interrelate. Then it becomes easier for staff to draw logical conclusions or connections between the resources the organization needs to deploy and the activities it must engage in to eventually arrive at its intended results.

A logic model has five basic components:

RESOURCES→ACTIVITIES→OUTPUTS→OUTCOMES→IMPACT

1. **Resources.** Sometimes referred to as inputs, the financial, human, organizational, or community investments in a program.

2. **Activities.** The events, processes, tools, or actions through which an organization deploys its resources, based on assumptions about how to achieve a program's goals.

3. **Outputs.** The immediate and direct results of the activities, such as the anticipated types or levels of service delivered to clients or members.

4. **Outcomes.** The ultimate goals of the program, such as specific changes in participants' knowledge, skills, or behaviors.

5. **Impact.** The fundamental and long-term consequences of delivering the outputs and achieving the outcomes. Years may go by before an organization, community, or system realizes the intended impact.

These components are linked by an "if...then..." chain of reasoning. For example:

- If we collaborate with another organization or a government agency, then we could sponsor an economic development conference (Resources —> Activities).

- If we sponsor the economic development conference, then we could provide 150 community leaders from around the state with the latest information on economic trends, demographic patterns, and infrastructure requirements for businesses (Activities —> Outputs).

- If we provide 150 participants with a high-quality educational experience, then they will return to their communities with ideas of how to attract new or expanded business, thus fulfilling our mission to promote economic growth (Outputs —> Outcomes).

- If various communities put some of these ideas to work successfully, then the state's overall economic health will improve (Outcomes —> Impact).

Evaluation figures into each component. Regarding Resources and Activities, for example, the staff might ask, "What aspects of our situation shape our ability to undertake this program?" to help guide program design and implementation. For Outcomes and Impact, the staff might ask, "What have we learned about undertaking this program?" and "What would we need to modify if we did this again in the future?"

To guard against the organization wasting its resources (time, money, staff, and so forth), the program must lead to the desired outcomes that justify doing it in the first place. To clarify those desired outcomes, many organizations essentially work backward through the logic model — they start with the ultimate outcomes or results, then backtrack to define the activities that must happen and identify the resources that must exist. This methodology, often referred to as "a theory of change," defines the preconditions required to achieve a specific goal.

Implicit in a theory of change are various assumptions that explain the connections in the logic model. In other words, staff members must be able to articulate their assumptions — ideally, supported by research — as to why a particular activity will lead to the desired outcome. If evaluation data prove those assumptions incorrect, then the logic model can be modified to reflect new assumptions about how to achieve the desired change.

TIP

Dashboards can be useful for staff as well as board members. Create more detailed dashboards for program directors so they can easily monitor the evolution and progress of specific programs.

WHAT TO DO WITH THE INFORMATION

Program evaluation results, including specific outcomes, should be communicated to the board, staff, current and potential users of the organization's programs and services, and funders. An organization should tailor the message and amount of information offered to individual stakeholder groups to match the involvement they have with the program. The more they've been involved, the more they'll want to know. If they've had little or no involvement, they will need and want only broad impact statements.

There is no need to wait for a program evaluation to be completed to report results. Dashboards are useful tools for reporting outcomes on an incremental basis at specific times (see Chapter 7). The chart below, from Lawrence M. Butler's book, *The Nonprofit Dashboard: A Tool for Tracking Progress* (BoardSource, 2007), illustrates how dashboard reporting can be integrated into the cycle of planning and evaluation. A one-page dashboard sheet, included from time to time in the information packet for a board meeting, is one way to update board members on evaluation progress. The dashboard outlines key indicators of organizational performance measures and features color-coded icons that show how the organization is performing. Used consistently, dashboards help the board monitor progress against the strategic plan.

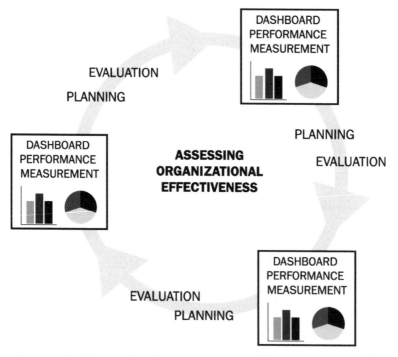

Communicating results from a program evaluation should also include the challenges faced and the results that were not achieved as planned. Reporting only good news can look suspicious. Funders, in particular, like to see that an organization can recognize and reflect upon its mistakes and adjust its strategies to respond to unintended consequences.

Communicating program results can yield the following benefits:

- tell the organization's story to funders, potential users, media, and other interested parties

- attract potential partners

- enhance public image and visibility

- recognize publicly a job well done

- provide direction to staff and volunteers and create clear priorities

Identifying and communicating the results of evaluation strengthens the link between planning and evaluation. The board of directors in particular must know about and understand the outcomes of an organization's efforts to achieve its mission, because outcomes must match an organization's mission, vision, and strategic goals. Program evaluation tells the board whether a program still fits within the organization's strategic framework. Program results can indicate whether the program is well implemented and suggest possible changes in current management or the next strategic plan.

QUESTIONS THE BOARD SHOULD ASK

1. When are the organization's programs evaluated? Is evaluation frequent enough?

2. What evaluation methods are used? What are the evaluation criteria?

3. Does staff provide evaluation results in the form of dashboards or other formats?

4. How do we use data from program evaluation in our decision making?

5. How do we use evaluation results externally to attract partners, enhance public image, and tell the organization's story?

CHAPTER 9
EVALUATING ORGANIZATIONAL EFFECTIVENESS

As the steward of an organization for the community, the board is responsible for assessing the organization's effectiveness. Deborah Linnell describes organizational effectiveness as "the capacity of an organization to sustain the people, strategies, learning, infrastructure, and resources it needs to continue to achieve its mission" (*Evaluation of Capacity Building: Lessons from the Field*, Alliance for Nonprofit Management, 2003).

Corporate boards spend much more time measuring performance at this level, both short-term and long-term, argues William Bowen, than do boards of nonprofit organizations (*Inside the Boardroom*, John Wiley & Sons, 1994). Corporate boards have always needed to keep an eye on the bottom line to maximize return on investment for shareholders. Nonprofit organizations, however, are asked more and more to document and assess results or bottom-line indicators so that funders and the public at large can determine whether the organization is achieving the kind of results its clients and constituents demand — and doing so efficiently and effectively.

Many nonprofit boards are used to monitoring financial performance and program progress, but fewer boards pay attention to the broader and more complex task of measuring their organizations' impact. Evaluating organizational effectiveness is directly linked to expressing and monitoring mission. In fact, it seems clear that a board can't know whether the organization is fulfilling its mission without an intentional commitment to assessing impact. Board and staff should work together to decide on critical indicators based on mission, vision, and strategic priorities, as well as a consideration of community needs, comparable organizations, and the operating environment.

◐✧ TIP

Some organizations find it truly difficult to measure impact. Hold a brainstorming session to identify unconventional methods for showing how you make a difference. To support your story, rely on testimonials, case studies, and funders' continuous support.

A BASIC FORMULA

This simple formula illustrates the components of an organizational evaluation:

> Internal effectiveness + external results = organizational effectiveness

Organizational effectiveness takes into account performance in a variety of organizational areas, including

- program impact and outcomes

- service coordination (including systems such as management information)

- financial stability

- staff qualifications, tenure, and turnover

- visibility (including the ability to get the word out and attract clients or audiences)

The SWOT analysis conducted during strategic planning (see Chapter 6) is an evaluation tool that can also contribute useful information (especially qualitative data) to an analysis of organizational effectiveness. Sometimes, in preparing for a SWOT analysis, an organization surveys its internal and external stakeholders about its strengths and weaknesses. The information external stakeholders provide can be more a matter of perception, but the information internal stakeholders provide highlight what is and is not working in an organization.

HOW ARE YOU DOING?

Five questions guide development of an organizational evaluation process:

1. *What do you currently measure?* There's no need to reinvent the wheel. Many organizations collect data from their Web sites, customer or constituent surveys, and other sources that can form the basis of ongoing measurement.

2. *What or who is driving the need for measurement?* Whether it's a new funder, the board chair, or the chief executive who's asking, being clear and honest about why you need information is the first step toward a positive, effective review of your programs or organization.

3. *Are you measuring "process" or "outcomes"?* Process focuses on what you do and how well you do it; outcomes identify the difference you make. This distinction is an important step toward confirming your vision of success and developing key indicators that reflect progress toward that vision.

4. *Is the information you collect mission-critical?* Some information is easy to quantify but ultimately says little about what you really accomplish as an organization. To avoid overwhelming staff with excessive "bean counting," narrow your scope to what's truly important — and relatively easy to obtain.

5. *Can you attribute your outcomes to your work?* Your mission is likely aimed at a long-term objective, such as improving the lives of people in your community. But what are the short-term goals that you hope to achieve first? For example, think about how your work increases awareness through education, promotion, or advocacy.

Source: Dan Baum, "Measuring Effectiveness 101," *Board Member®* (November/December 2006)

Two other types of evaluation, far from being separate and distinct processes, are linked to organizational success. They involve assessing the chief executive's performance and assessing the board's performance.

Robert D. Herman and his research colleagues David Renz and Richard Heimovics have found that when board members and chief executives put time and effort into building skills that are known to contribute to effective boards, the effectiveness of the organization is likely to improve as well ("Board Practices and Board Effectiveness in Local Nonprofit Organizations," *Nonprofit Management and Leadership,* Summer 1997). Board self-assessment helps board members reflect with candor on how well they are meeting their responsibilities, helps the board focus on areas needing improvement, and motivates the board to work for the benefit of the organization and those it serves.

Similarly, evaluation of the chief executive helps strengthen the person's performance and ultimately contributes to the effectiveness of the organization as a whole. The organization's overall performance is a critical part of the chief executive's leadership role; when executive performance does not meet expectations, there can be an adverse impact on the organization.

WHAT TO DO WITH THE INFORMATION

Ultimately, organizations have to decide what success looks like for them. What goals have they established during their planning cycle that outline that success? What evidence and results will indicate that they have been effective? Organizational effectiveness is the extent to which an organization has met its stated goals and objectives — the key link to strategic planning — and how well it performed in the process.

Quantitative measurements don't always tell the whole story of success. Sometimes progress toward mission is best revealed in the compelling stories about the difference an organization is making in its community. Here's an example from "Making Progress on Mission," in the March/April 2008 issue of *Board Member*®:

> At Dress for Success Indianapolis, our mission is to "empower women to enter and thrive in the workforce with style, self-confidence, and hope for the future." How do we know we're achieving that? At our most recent annual fundraiser, 10 women, all clients of our

organization, stood on stage in front of 800 people and told stories about how our organization had had a positive impact on their lives. They told the audience how we had helped them and continue to help them on the road to self-sufficiency; how we have helped them gain confidence; how they genuinely cherish the ongoing support they receive from us; and how, without this support, their journeys to self-sufficiency might not be achievable. With or without numbers, these stories prove to me that we are making progress on our mission.

The information a board obtains from an organizational assessment becomes part of the evaluative data that inform the next strategic planning process, seamlessly supporting a continuous cycle of planning and evaluation. An organization may consider examining its overall effectiveness every three to five years, thus corresponding with its strategic planning cycle. In doing so, the board has established a natural plan to assess progress on the journey to its envisioned future.

PITFALL

If you emphasize quantitative measures at the expense of qualitative measures, the staff will devote too much time to "bean counting" and not enough time to figuring out creative ways to demonstrate value and show meaningful outcomes.

QUESTIONS THE BOARD SHOULD ASK

1. Do we take responsibility as a board for assessing the organization's effectiveness?

2. Are we as a board committed to assessing our own effectiveness?

3. Do we regularly assess the performance of the chief executive?

CONCLUSION
TOWARD A BETTER BOARD

We hope you're inspired by the ideas we've offered. Most of all, we hope you take away the message that mission, planning, and evaluation are seamlessly integrated, not separate functions — and powerful motivators that influence and strengthen the work of the board. As creators, keepers, and advancers of the mission, board members have a serious responsibility. It's up to the board to make sure the mission stays clear, vibrant, and valid over time and to commit to a continuous cycle of strategic planning and evaluation.

THIRTEEN THINGS TO REMEMBER

In a crowded field of competitor organizations, nonprofits must prove their worth again and again. They must do more than tell a compelling story. They must prove their value to a community by achieving their intended results. In taking on that task, reflect on the guidance outlined in this book. Revisit it often. And remember these points about mission, planning, and evaluation:

1. On a regular basis, examine the values of your organization, and then evaluate your mission and its expression in all your materials to see if your values are evident.

2. Be diligent and intentional about your board recruitment process, even if it is going well. Be sure it is thorough and that new board members are recruited not only for their expertise and connections but also for their belief in your mission.

3. Make sure that orientations for new board members (and continuing board members) are the highest-quality mission-revealing experiences.

4. Immerse the board regularly in feedback from a satisfied community by e-mail and in person; devote a moment or two at each board meeting to sharing information about someone who was touched by your organization's efforts. Be sure management uses the same approach with staff meetings.

5. In donor and fund development, talk about investment — about the need you are meeting (your mission), not the need you have.

6. Build relationships around shared values, common vision, and a common understanding of mission. If you build the relationships, the money (and the volunteers) will come.

7. Use strategic planning as an opportunity to continue your dreams and visions for the organization.

8. Remember that there may be times when it is not advisable to engage in a strategic planning process.

9. Embrace the potential to build relationships and enhance communication among board, staff, and stakeholders during the planning process.

10. Capitalize on the diverse experience of board members during planning, and make sure each person is invited to contribute.

11. Use evaluation as an opportunity for internal learning that helps strengthen programs and services.

12. Put the information gained during evaluation to good use for the benefit of the organization and its constituents.

13. Be mindful of board and staff roles in evaluation. It is primarily a staff responsibility, but the board must make sure it happens and monitor the results.

The responsibility for mission, planning, and evaluation should be an inspiration, not a burden. When it is understood and used in the way described in this book, it can engage board leadership and increase advocacy. And the impact? Incredible — on the board member, the organization, and the community.

SUGGESTED RESOURCES

Angelica, Emil. *Fieldstone Alliance Nonprofit Guide to Crafting Effective Mission and Vision Statements.* St. Paul, MN: Fieldstone Alliance, 2001.

This handbook will help your organization develop (or revise) mission and vision statements that bring focus and direction to your work. Easy-to-follow steps show how to build ownership for the mission and vision statements among board and staff and create a common understanding of your organization's goals. This guide includes definitions of mission and vision statements, a process to develop a mission and vision statement, and worksheets to guide the process.

Barry, Bryan W. *Strategic Planning Workbook for Nonprofit Organizations.* St. Paul, MN: Fieldstone Alliance, 2001.

Strategic planning is a tool for finding the best future for your organization and the best path to reach that destination. This workbook offers practical guidance through five planning steps, with step-by-step worksheets for developing the plan, involving others in the process, and measuring results.

BoardSource. *Assessment for Nonprofit Governing Boards: Online Tool.* Washington, DC: BoardSource.

This online self-assessment tool helps nonprofit boards determine how well they are carrying out their responsibilities and identifies areas that need improvement. Board members complete confidential online questionnaires to evaluate the board's performance as well as their own contributions. Their responses help identify the strengths and weaknesses of the current board with questions focused on 10 key areas of board responsibility.

BoardSource. *The Nonprofit Board Answer Book: A Practical Guide for Board Members and Chief Executives, Second Edition.* Washington, DC: BoardSource, 2007.

The second edition of this best-selling resource contains 80 questions and answers that provide information about board structure and process, meetings, board composition, orientation, board – staff relations, financial management, and more. Written in an easy-to-use format, it includes action steps, examples, and worksheets.

BoardSource. *The Source: Twelve Principles of Governance That Power Exceptional Boards.* Washington, DC: BoardSource, 2005.

Exceptional boards add significant value to their organizations, making discernible differences in their advance on mission. *The Source: Twelve Principles of Governance That Power Exceptional Boards* defines governance not as dry, obligatory compliance, but as a creative and collaborative process that supports chief executives, engages board members, and furthers the causes they all serve.

The Source enables nonprofit boards to operate at the highest and best use of their collective capacity. Aspirational in nature, these principles offer chief executives a description of an empowered board that is a strategic asset to be leveraged. They provide board members with a vision of what is possible and a way to add lasting value to the organizations they lead.

Bruner, Charles. "So You Think You Need Some Help? Making Effective Use of Technical Assistance." National Center for Service Integration, 1993. www.cfpciowa.org/publications/ccbs/index.htm

This resource brief is designed to help organizations develop productive consulting relationships that suit their needs and the needs of their constituencies. Topics include the reasons for seeking technical assistance from a consultant, the types of assistance offered, and issues in choosing a consultant.

Butler, Lawrence M. *The Nonprofit Dashboard: A Tool for Tracking Progress*. Washington, DC: BoardSource, 2007.

Board oversight involves more than just reading financial statements, and nonprofit boards don't always know how nor have the opportunity to provide adequate programmatic oversight. This resource explains how to use dashboard reports to communicate critical information to the board in a concise, visual, compelling way. It addresses where a dashboard fits in to planning and evaluation and highlights the important partnership between staff and board in creating and effectively using a dashboard program.

Connolly, Paul M. *Navigating the Organizational Lifecycle: A Capacity-Building Guide for Nonprofit Leaders*. Washington, DC: BoardSource, 2006.

Knowing how to assess a nonprofit organization's stage of development helps leaders align capacities, manage organizational transitions, and anticipate future challenges. This book introduces strategies for making the case to funders for capacity-building support. It also makes it easier for board members and chief executives to assess where their organizations are in their lifecycle and help determine if capacities are appropriate to the current stage of development.

Eadie, Doug. *Boards That Work: A Practical Guide to Building Effective Association Boards*. Washington, DC: ASAE, 1995.

An effective approach to board relations is based on flexibility, openness, and commitment to innovation. This book challenges the conventional wisdom surrounding board organization and training and applies this vision to the board's mission, membership, leadership training, performance management, structure, strategic planning, public relations, retreats, implementation of change, and more.

Ingram, Richard T. *Ten Basic Responsibilities of Nonprofit Boards, Second Edition.* Washington, DC: BoardSource, 2008.

This revised edition of a classic bestseller explores the 10 core areas of board responsibility, including determining mission and purpose, ensuring effective planning, and participating in fundraising. It is an ideal reference for drafting job descriptions, assessing board performance, and orienting board members.

Kocsis, Deborah L., and Susan A. Waechter. *Driving Strategic Planning: A Nonprofit Executive's Guide.* Washington, DC: BoardSource, 2003.

Executives who have decided to embark on strategic planning but don't know where to begin will value this basic overview. It explains how to work with the staff and board to assess the readiness of the organization and prepare for strategic planning. Included are a variety of approaches for dealing with common issues and overcoming organizational resistance to beginning the process, along with a review of the fundamental components of a strategic plan, from mission and vision to environmental scan and competitive analysis.

Lawrence, Barbara, and Outi Flynn. *The Nonprofit Policy Sampler, Second Edition.* Washington, DC: BoardSource, 2006.

The Nonprofit Policy Sampler is designed to help board and staff leaders advance their organizations, make better collective decisions, and guide individual actions and behaviors. This tool provides key elements and practical tips for 48 topic areas, along with more than 240 sample policies, job descriptions, committee charters, codes of ethics, board member agreements, mission and vision statements, and more. Each topic includes anywhere from two to 10 sample documents so that nonprofit leaders can select an appropriate sample from which to start drafting or revising their own policy. All samples are professionally and legally reviewed. Samples are included on CD-ROM.

Mintz, Joshua, and Jane Pierson. *Assessment of the Chief Executive*. Washington, DC: BoardSource, 2007.

Assessing the chief executive is one of the board's primary governance responsibilities and is critical to the success of the executive and the organization as a whole. This tool clarifies the chief executive's responsibilities, job expectations, and annual goals; captures the board's perception of the executive's strengths, limitations, and overall performance; and fosters growth and development of the chief executive and the organization.

York, Peter J. *Learning as We Go: Making Evaluation Work for Everyone. A Briefing Paper for Funders and Nonprofits*. TCC Group, 2003. www.tccgrp.com/pubs/evaluation.php

This paper explains the difference between evaluation for accountability and evaluation for learning — a collaborative approach that the author calls "evaluative learning." Information and tools help take small and large organizations to the next level as a learning and capacity-building tool.

ABOUT THE AUTHORS

KAY SPRINKEL GRACE

Kay Sprinkel Grace, CFRE, is a San Francisco–based organizational consultant, providing workshops and consultation to local, regional, national, and international organizations in strategic planning, case and board development, staff development, and other issues related to leadership of the fundraising process. From March 2004 to June 2007, she was principal external consultant to the Corporation for Public Broadcasting's Major Giving Initiative. Other clients include San Francisco Museum of Modern Art; Internews; Santa Barbara Art Museum; Kronos Quartet; Family Violence Prevention Fund; Sutter Health Foundations; St. Joseph Health System Foundations; California Council of Land Trusts; St. Dominic's Church, San Francisco; Boys & Girls Clubs of the Peninsula; Loma Linda University and Medical Center.

Her B.A. (Communications-Journalism) and M.A. (Education) are from Stanford University, where she served as the first woman volunteer chair of the Stanford Fund. She was also national volunteer chair of the Keystone Program ($10,000 - $100,000 gifts) for Stanford's $1.1 billion Centennial Campaign, which raised $72 million. She has received Stanford's highest award for volunteer service, the Gold Spike, as well as its Associates' Award, Outstanding Achievement Award, Award of Merit, and Centennial Medal. She also has been recognized as Outstanding Fund Raising Executive by the Golden Gate Chapter of the National Society of Fund Raising Executives (now AFP) in 1992.

Grace is the author of six books: *Beyond Fund Raising: New Strategies for Nonprofit Innovation and Investment* (John Wiley & Sons, 1997; second edition, 2005); *High Impact Philanthropy: How Donors, Boards, and Nonprofit Organizations Can Transform Communities,* co-author, with Alan Wendroff (John Wiley & Sons, 2001); *Over Goal! What You Must Know to Excel at Fundraising Today* (Emerson & Church, 2003); *The Ultimate Board Member's Book* (Emerson & Church, 2003); *Fundraising*

Mistakes That Bedevil All Boards (Emerson & Church, 2004); *AAA Boards*, (2008); and of the booklet, (*The Board's Role in Setting and Advancing the Mission* (BoardSource, 2003).) A regular columnist for the bimonthly publication *Contributions*, she has also contributed chapters to *Achieving Excellence in Fund Raising* by Henry A. Rosso (1987 and 2003), *Taking Fund Raising Seriously*, and *Taking Trusteeship Seriously*.

She serves on the advisory board of the John W. Gardner Center for Youth and Their Communities at Stanford University, and previously served on the boards of the Djerassi Resident Artist Program (Woodside, Calif), the Women's Philanthropy Institute, and the Advisory Board for the University of San Francisco Institute for Nonprofit Organization Management. She lives in San Francisco and is passionate about her children and grandchildren, philanthropy, writing, travel, and her photography.

AMY MCCLELLAN

Amy McClellan is executive director of the Nonprofit Academic Centers Council (NACC) housed at the Mandel Center for Nonprofit Organizations at Case Western Reserve University. As a membership association, NACC's mission is to support academic centers devoted to the study of the nonprofit sector, philanthropy, and voluntary action in order to advance education, research, and practice in the field.

Prior to joining NACC as its first executive director, McClellan was manager of school and community partnerships for The Cleveland Orchestra. She has more than 20 years of experience in the nonprofit sector in advancing degrees of management in both program and resource development. She has also co-facilitated strategic planning and strategic alliance processes for nonprofit organizations and has been a program consultant for The Cleveland Foundation, working on behalf of the foundation on a number of special projects.

McClellan holds a B.A. from The Colorado College and a master's degree in Nonprofit Organizations from Case Western Reserve University in Cleveland, receiving academic honors upon graduation from both institutions. She has been a member of a research team at the Mandel Center for Nonprofit Organizations, examining strategic alliances in the nonprofit sector. She has co-authored *Nonprofit Strategic Alliances Case Studies: Lessons from the Trenches,* a publication of the Mandel Center; *The Nonprofit Board's Role in Planning and Evaluation,* (BoardSource) and an article "Arts Organizations and the Pursuit of Persistent Presence" in the journal *Nonprofit Management Leadership.*

JOHN A. YANKEY, PH.D.

Dr. John A. Yankey is the Leonard W. Mayo Professor Emeritus at the Mandel School of Applied Social Sciences and Mandel Center for Nonprofit Organizations at Case Western Reserve University. Yankey continues to teach in the areas of strategic planning, developing strategic nonprofit partnerships/alliances, and legislative and political processes. During his 35 years at Case Western Reserve University, he has administered a number of statewide training programs, served in a variety of administrative positions, and carried out state legislative liaison responsibilities as Special Assistant to the President. During the last 15 years, he has been heavily involved in both studying strategic alliances or partnerships and in facilitating nonprofit organizations through feasibility studies to establish such alliances.

Yankey has published a number of articles in public and nonprofit management journals throughout his career. In 1991, he co-edited *Skills for Effective Human Services Management,* a popular text in social work management education programs throughout the United States. In 1996, he co-authored *Building a Strong Foundation: Fundraising for Nonprofits.* In 1998, he co-edited a new nonprofit management text titled *Skills for Effective Management of Nonprofit Organizations.* In 2001, he co-authored two workbooks on developing strategic alliances: *Merging Non-profit Organizations: The Art & Science of the Deal* and *Nonprofit Strategic Alliances Case Studies: Lessons from the Trenches.* In 2002, Yankey co-authored *The Nonprofit Board's Role in Planning and Evaluation* for BoardSource. In 2004, he co-authored three case studies on the role of trust in developing nonprofit strategic alliances. In 2005, he was co-author of a comprehensive overview of studies on nonprofit strategic alliance development, which was published in the *Jossey-Bass Handbook for Nonprofit Management and Leadership.* In 2006, he co-edited and co-authored several chapters in *Effectively Managing Nonprofit Organizations.*